'The stories in *Hard Pushed* highlight the bravery
of our midwives, and the women they care for.'
Christie Watson, author of
The Language of Kindness

'A "love letter" to midwives everywhere – which
brings the maternity ward to life in all its gory,
humorous and touching glory.'
Telegraph

'Heart-rending, inspiring and funny, *Hard Pushed*
brings alive the world of midwifery in all its
complexity and radiates love and respect
for women.'
Professor Lesley Page CBE, former president
of the Royal College of Midwives

'You will laugh, cry and not quite believe what you
read. I loved every word.'
Sun

'*Hard Pushed* charts a midwife's most personal
moments of triumph and devastating loss in a way
that expands our understanding and gratitude to
them. Leah Hazard's "microdoses" of love are exactly
what we need at a time of transforming intensity.
It is her capacity to love and give so personally
to the many thousands of women she has worked
with which imbues this book with its power.'
Julia Samuel, author of *Grief Works*

'Not only powerful but well written too . . . a
worthwhile addition to a genre fast becoming
as crowded as a busy maternity unit.'
Daily Express

HARD PUSHED
A Midwife's Story

Leah Hazard

arrow books

1 3 5 7 9 10 8 6 4 2

Arrow Books
20 Vauxhall Bridge Road
London SW1V 2SA

Arrow Books is part of the Penguin Random House group of companies
whose addresses can be found at global.penguinrandomhouse.com

Penguin
Random House
UK

First published in the United Kingdom by Hutchinson in 2019
First published by Arrow Books in 2020

www.penguin.co.uk

A CIP catalogue record for this book is available
from the British Library.

ISBN 9781787464216

Pri ... S.p.A.

P ... ture
for ... made

'There must be those among whom we can sit down
and weep and still be counted as warriors.'
Adrienne Rich

Contents

Author's Note

The events described in this book are based on my life, experiences and recollections. To preserve patient confidentiality and the privacy of colleagues, names, places and all identifying features have been changed. The stories told are not based on any one specific patient or individual; rather, they are a selection of composite characters drawing from my various experiences. Any similarities are purely coincidental.

Where It Begins

Another night, another vagina.

It's not unusual for me to spend the night between a stranger's legs. Sometimes two or three strangers in the space of twelve hours. Tonight is a bit different, though. It's 3.42 a.m. and things aren't going to plan. Sitting in point-blank range of this particular vagina feels like staring down the barrel of a gun. Birth is inherently risky, a kind of physiological Russian roulette, but every midwife prays that she'll dodge the bullet.

'I can't do it,' wails a disembodied voice. At the same time, a slick patch of dark hair looms into view in front of me. 'You *are* doing it, and you *will* do it,' I call up to the voice. I glance quickly at the clock on the wall and then say quietly, to myself, *03.44, vertex visible.* I will need to write a detailed report of all of these times and events later, when the blood-stained paper drapes have been bagged and tagged, a tray of tea and biscuits sits on the window sill and the baby has arrived safely. *If* the baby arrives safely.

Another contraction powers through the woman in front of me; her open legs judder and shake; the small circle of hair becomes negligibly wider as the baby's head is nudged a millimetre closer to the outside world. *03.46*, I note silently. *Vertex advancing.* 'For fuck's sake,' comes the voice from the top of the bed. 'Make it stop. Pull it out, cut it out, I don't fucking care any more.' So much effort for so little progress. Beads of sweat are dripping down the bridge of my nose now; the room is dark apart from one spotlight blazing a single white beam between my patient's legs. My hands are gloved and sterile; unable to touch anything but the woman in front of me. I let the sweat trickle down my nose, my chin, the back of my neck.

'That perineum's tight,' says another voice, from over my shoulder this time. Mary, the midwife who answered my buzzer for help with the birth, is looking on. 'It's not stretching out,' she says, echoing my own unspoken fears as another contraction shakes the woman's body and the top of the baby's head pushes in vain against this thick band of skin.

Tick, tick, tick … tick … tick. Mary and I tense in unison as the monitor picking up the baby's heartbeat slows, becoming irregular, sounding a familiar warning. *03.49, audible deceleration to 96 beats per minute.* This is the drumroll we dread.

'Your baby's getting a bit tired,' I say cautiously to the woman on the bed.

'That makes two of us,' retorts the voice, ragged and weary now.

A smaller contraction nudges the baby's head; again, the taut skin holds it back.

'You're going to have to do an episiotomy,' whispers Mary. I glance over at the tray of instruments just within reach on the metal trolley to my right. Cord clamps, water, cotton wool, sanitary pads. A small, stubby pair of scissors for cutting the cord and another, longer pair of scissors with short, straight blades, for cutting through skin and muscle. Recently, the hospital changed suppliers and, coincidentally or not, most of the scissors in these trays have been blunt. Cheaper, blunter: the staff could have T-shirts made with this slogan, I muse, as the fetal monitor's rhythm stutters and slows. My tired mind veers back to the situation at hand, and I resume the documentation in my head. *15.51*, I think, and then draw an imaginary line through my mental note. My brain is clearly wishing it were a day shift. *03.51*, I start again. *Fetal heart 108 bpm, decels persist. Preparing for episiotomy.*

'We might have to make a wee cut,' I call brightly to the voice at the top of the bed. 'Just to help this baby out.' So many things in midwifery are 'wee' – a wee cut, a wee tear, a wee bleed, the latter used to describe anything from a trickle to a torrent. Euphemisms are one of our many small mercies: we learn early on to downplay and dissemble. The brutality of birth is often self-evident; there is little need to elaborate.

The monitor continues its erratic backbeat, the baby's pulse now sitting at seventy-four beats per minute – roughly half of what it should be – and it's not coming back up to a reasonable baseline in between contractions. Mary passes me the scissors. A glass bottle of lidocaine catches the light at the edge of the trolley, but the baby's heartbeat is slowing, and there may not be time to inject the local anaesthetic.

'Fuck, fuck, fuck.' A voice. I'm no longer sure if it's the patient's or the one in my own head. Hand quivering with nerves and caffeine, I loop two fingers just inside the band of skin, creating a pocket between skin and baby where I know I can cut. Technical term: a mediolateral episiotomy. Reality: a deep bite into tender tissue at the angle of eight o'clock, an outrageous insult to the pelvic floor, but an instantaneous way to ease a baby's troubled passage. I hate doing this. I hate cutting women, I hate the pain this will cause them for days, if not weeks, to come, and I hate knowing that in about half an hour's time, all going well, I will have to repair my own handiwork. Just when the patient begins to relax, lying back with her baby scrabbling happily on her chest, I will have to find a second wind and begin round two. Scrub up, gown up, new instruments, curved needle and spooled suture poised in mid-air to fix the damage done.

I raise my scissors. An almighty wave surges through the woman and the baby's head lunges forward. 'Jesus, Mary and aaaaaaaaaah,' roars a voice. *Please let these scissors be sharp*, says the quieter, but no less urgent, voice in my head. *Please let this baby come. Please let it be OK.* And finally, the urgent, daily prayer of midwives everywhere: *Please let me keep my job and not be struck off when something horrible happens and please, please, please let my bladder hold*

*for at least another hour until this is over and done
with.*

It's not even 4 a.m. yet. I've been awake for almost
twenty-four hours. Scissors meet flesh. How did I get
here?

Notes on Bowling Balls, and Other Birth Stories

I learned about childbirth from Mike Katz, second-place winner of Mr. Olympia 1976 (Over 200-pound Division), and holder of other such illustrious titles as Mr. Insurance City (ninth place, 1963), Mr. Universe Tall (third place, 1973) and Mr. America Tall & Overall (fourth place, 1970). Mike Katz – or Mr Katz, as he was known to me during my high-school years – was a veteran bodybuilder, teacher and ice hockey coach with a record-busting 60-inch chest in his prime and hulking biceps so large that he had to strut the school corridors with his arms held at a jaunty distance from his torso.

Weightlifting and muscle mass may not have been on my radar, but all students were required to take 'health' class, which was taught by – guess who – Mr Katz. Most sessions were based around the school's collection of educational films – cautionary tales that covered a range of topics from drink driving to 'sex ed'.

The real *pièce de résistance*, however, was the Birth Video. When the big moment arrived, Mr Katz stood at the front of the class, solemnly aimed the remote control at the VCR, and with very little indication of the labour that must have gone before, the Birth Video whirred into life. The screen flickered and the static cleared to reveal a close-up shot of a baby's head crowning between a woman's outstretched and stir-ruped legs. There were screams, there was some blood and there was the baby's head, getting bigger and bigger as it distended this poor woman's vulva to seem-ingly impossible dimensions. Boys shifted in their seats, unsure whether to feel disgusted or aroused by this rare close-up of unadorned ladygarden. Girls crossed their legs and winced but couldn't look away. Was this our future? How would we do it? When would the screaming stop? And there, holding forth at the front of the class with dancing eyes and an incredulous grin, was Mr Katz.

'Would you look at the size of that, kids!' he exclaimed. 'It's like a freaking bowling ball.'

Mr Katz may have been an unlikely guru of obstetric knowledge, but something else about the Birth Video stayed with me for years. In spite of the film's brutal aesthetic, I couldn't help sharing some of Mr Katz's sense of awe. A truth had been revealed to me: birth *is* amazing. Sometimes violent, sometimes shocking, but amazing. How a head that size can fit through a slender sleeve of vagina is the kind of conundrum that can't help but puzzle and fascinate even the most cynical observer. But the real fascination for sixteen-year-old me was the question of whether women could 'do' birth in other ways? Sitting, standing, even smiling, laughing? What was happening to the rest of that woman in the video – to her face, her heart, her mind – above that cropped shot of a disembodied vulva?

The next years went by with only the most fleeting thought of the mysteries of childbirth until finally, as a newlywed at the age of twenty-five, I began to find the notion of having a baby with my straight-talking, ginger-bearded Scottish husband irresistibly attractive. When that notion materialised into two blue lines on a pregnancy test, I embraced maternity with all of the gusto I had previously used to avoid it. I read the books, I scoured the Internet and, like a dutiful little mother-to-be, I attended my first antenatal – or 'Parentcraft' – classes.

'Parentcraft' makes it sound like a quaintly arti-sanal activity, something you might find in the prospectus of a community arts centre today, next to beekeeping, basket weaving, latte-making and the like. The reality was a bit different. Our destination: a windowless room in the basement of the local mater-nity hospital full of equally clueless, wide-eyed couples. Just as I had done all those years ago in Mr Katz's classroom, I sat down and waited for the Wisdom to be imparted.

For the next hour and a half, an older midwife with cropped silver hair and mischievously sparkling eyes held forth with great enthusiasm, gesticulating wildly at the anatomical illustrations displayed on easels at the front of the room. The uterus was depicted in scarlet red, the bladder was blue and the vagina a delicately ribbed rose, the whole reproductive system curled in on itself like some exotically whorled sea creature. The heat in the room became foggily tropical as the lesson continued and, this being winter in Scotland, everyone's wet woollens began to take on the distinct aroma of damp dog. A battery of fetal kicks sent a wave of nausea up my throat and my vision tunnelled as I started to slide down the chair.

I was clearly Not Cut Out for This. Panic and doubt followed the nausea and shame – if I couldn't even handle Parentcraft, how would I cope with labour, birth and the inevitable bowling-ball moment?

Between them, my daughters' births ended up running the gamut of obstetric experience: one emergency Caesarean section after a long, obstructed labour, and one home birth so unexpectedly quick that my husband had caught the baby before the midwife even arrived. How could two births have been so different? It felt like the only common denominator was a baby, but each event had brought me to the edge of my body and mind's capabilities. Even with the benefit of hindsight, Parentcraft and personal experience, I was still stumped. How did it happen? How could billions of women follow infinitely different journeys to the same destination? Was there a way to make more of these journeys joyful and fulfilling, and could those skills be taught, or learned? And if so, did I even have what it took to learn those dark arts – me, with my almost total lack of practical skills, my catastrophic lack of hand–eye coordination and my quasi-comical shortage of common sense? The questions planted by the Birth Video all those years ago had become urgent, real and compelling. I was finding my current job in television less fulfilling with each passing day and had flirted with the idea of retraining for a while, but until recently, my reluctance to go back to school had overshadowed my interest in midwifery. As my girls began to grow up and a new career seemed increasingly plausible, the balance tipped. I started to think that maybe, just maybe, there existed a parallel universe in which I could be that midwife who helped women get through pregnancy and birth with dignity (and pelvic floor) intact.

The interview process for my local midwifery course was a combination of practical skill and intense psychological pressure (which, I would later realise, was excellent preparation for midwifery itself). Two lecturers ushered me into an office and asked me a range of relatively standard questions, the answers to which I gave with ease; it was enjoyable to ramble on about autonomy, advocacy and empowerment to such a receptive audience. A doddle, I thought, as the women nodded encouragingly. What was all the fuss about?

Then the tone of the interview changed dramatically. I had been warned about the dreaded Maths Test, but nothing could prepare me for the bolt of pure, unadulterated fear that shot through my heart as the interviewers sat me down at a small desk in the corner of the room. On the top was a sheet of maths problems designed to mimic the kinds of calculations a midwife might encounter in her daily work. I should make it clear at this point that arithmetic has never been my strong point. I could barely work out the tip for a meal and, even now, every drug calculation brings me out in a cold sweat. I find myself double- and triple-checking, especially at the end of a night shift, when simple sums might as well be Nobel-level astrophysics.

Nevertheless, I drew a deep breath, put pen to paper, and smiled as if I began every day with a refreshing round of algebraic equations. Lesson number one to the novice midwife: midwifery is one part skill, umpteen parts Ballsing It Out. To this day, I'm convinced that my admission to the midwifery course had less to do with my numeracy skills and more to do with my ability to do sums under scrutiny for twenty minutes without actually soiling my pants.

Student Midwife Hazard:
She's Doing It

My first placement in the hospital's labour ward began with a night shift. I drove into the hospital car park, switched the engine off and sat clutching the steering wheel, rigid with fear, staring at the building in front of me. The sky was moonless, but the maternity unit's windows cast a yellow glow on the clusters of bath-robed smokers huddling outside, and the building itself appeared to hum with the frantic energy of a giant, oestrogen-driven generator. I shivered and chewed the inside of my cheek as I watched shadowy figures dart across windows on every floor, some trailing oversized balloons, some rushing to answer distant call bells.

Of course, my first shift in the hospital had been preceded by hours of rigorous preparation. No, I had not been revising the mechanisms of childbirth by poring over my notes from the last few weeks, nor had I been simulating delivery manoeuvres with a doll and pelvis. But I had taken a monumentally long time doing my make-up, hoping that every last sweep of blusher and flick of eyeliner could somehow conceal the underlying layer of abject terror. I had done all-nighters in the past, but none of them had required me to save a life, or repair ravaged flesh. I couldn't see how I would pull off these seemingly superhuman feats without divine intervention or the aid of substances that I could only imagine might be frowned upon by my mentors.

(Intervening experience has taught me that a startling number of health-care professionals are only too happy to throw themselves headlong into the vortex of substance abuse, using whatever means necessary to counteract the permanent state of jet lag induced by shift work and emotional exhaustion.)

Although I am now an expert at self-medicating with entirely legal uppers (coffee) and downers (a glass or several of gum-numbingly cold white wine) depending on where I am in my working week, I had anticipated my first night shift in a state of panicked confusion. How would I stay awake? When would I eat? *What* would I eat? I knew I should be getting three breaks in my twelve-and-a-quarter-hour shift, but does one eat breakfast at 10 p.m., lunch at 1 a.m. and dinner at 6 a.m., or the complete opposite? During the preceding week, I had spent hours packing a huge bag with a variety of neatly clip-locked tubs full of meals and snacks that could suit any combination or permutation of appetite and time. Anyone watching me lug my cargo of energy bars, fried rice, fruit salads and Frazzles across the hospital car park that evening would surely have thought that I was heading to a prolonged stay as an inpatient rather than a single shift as a student.

Hoisting my bag higher over my shoulder, I passed a low, squat sculpture of a pregnant woman by the building's front entrance; her ovoid bump was sleek and gleaming even in the dark, her face expressionless as she watched me disappear through the revolving doors and onwards to the staff changing room.

In some ways, this area of a maternity unit is a great equaliser: whereas the clichéd advice for calming one's nerves at a big event is to 'picture them all naked', the changing room allows the panicked, novice midwife to see her new colleagues quite literally naked. That ward sister who barked at you and made you cry? She's wearing day-of-the-week pants. The auxiliary who told you off for making a mess when you knotted your bin bags instead of tying them in the regulation 'swan neck'? A luxuriant bikini line and a lacy thong that leaves little to the imagination. Standing amidst the lockers before that first shift, I looked at the women around me in various states of undress – all shapes and sizes, some with dimpled flesh, some sleek, some with immaculately coiffured and back-teased ponytails, some looking as though they'd been dragged through the proverbial hedge – and told myself, *They're just women, like you. They're no different. They all had to start somewhere. It's fine.*

My confidence was short-lived. As I sifted through the scrubs heaped in jumbled piles by the door, I realised that the only sizes available were XXL or XXXL. Now, whilst two children have certainly left their indelible marks on my body, I don't need a uniform that could accommodate half the hospital's staff in a single trouser leg. It was something of a miracle when I finally found a set that wasn't ink- or bloodstained; I slipped the tent-like top over my head and pulled the trouser drawstring tight round my waist.

A cluster of women was gathered in front of a mirror, chattering cheerfully in a misty cloud of deodorant and perfume. I stood at their backs and gazed at my reflection, looking every inch the clown

I felt on the inside. The supersized trousers dragged on the floor, and the V-neck of my scrub top dipped low enough to give any inquisitive onlookers a glimpse of my greying 'work' bra. A clock above the mirror read 7.22 p.m.; my shift started at 7.30 p.m., so there was no delaying my shameful debut in this circus. I pinned my name badge to my chest – Student Midwife Hazard – and winced in anticipation of the inevitable jokes that my 'dangerous' name would attract throughout the rest of my new career. (Though, during the odd bout of sleep-deprived delirium in the years to come, I will admit to having answered patients' buzzers by breezily pulling their curtains back and declaring, 'Midwife Hazard, at your cervix!')

I tailed a group of midwives through the hospital's labyrinthine interior and up in the lift until a tired 'ding' announced our arrival at the labour ward on the fourth floor. The lift spilled its chattering contents into a small foyer, where a wheelchair bearing a 'WARD 68 – DO NOT REMOVE' tag on its handles had been parked beneath a peeling trio of breastfeeding posters. The midwives turned right, moving in a throng of burbling gossip and hairspray through a set of double doors; I slipped in after them like a stowaway as the doors began to shut. Inside, cool light bounced off gleaming floors, and the air seemed thinner, somehow; a blend of disinfectant and the acrid tang of blood. I breathed deep and followed on to the 'bunker', a room so named because all plans for obstetric engagements originated in its cramped, windowless confines. One wall was covered in handwritten signs for shift swaps, union meetings and '70s tribute nights, while the opposite wall held two large whiteboards on which were scrawled the names of every patient in the department and a coded summary of each woman's progress so far. At the start of each shift, midwives gather in the bunker and wait for the senior charge midwife – the labour ward 'sister' – to allocate patients. It's a lottery that can determine whether the next twelve-and-a-quarter hours will be a soul-destroying slog that ends in the operating theatre or a joyful journey towards an easy, euphoric birth, with a grateful couple waving you off in floods of happy tears.

Tonight's sister was tall with a short shock of fiery red hair and a long beak of a nose. She peered down at her staff – nine midwives and one terrified student – then back at the board, mentally matching up staff to patients, before barking out the night's orders.

'Room three, para one at thirty-eight weeks, insulin-controlled Type One diabetic on a sliding scale, six centimetres, malposition ... Luisa.' The sister nodded to a midwife sitting by the door, who cursed just loudly enough for us all to hear and ducked out of the bunker towards room three.

'Room Six, prim at term plus twelve, IOL for post-dates, high BMI, failed epidural, baby with a known VSD, two centimetres, on Syntocinon ... Jenny.' A young midwife with a tight, glossy ponytail stood up and tumbled through the door like a paratrooper hurling herself out of a plane into enemy territory.

What was this language being spoken? You, dear reader, have the benefit of the glossary at the back of this book to guide you through the jargon – a quick browse and you could bluff your way through a basic ward round. For me, though – newly minted Student Midwife Hazard, quaking in her trainers – the sister's orders fell on cloth ears. I could just about decipher the words 'prim' (first-timer, in obstetric shorthand) and 'para one' (mother of one), but the intervening tumult of abbreviations and complications was virtually incomprehensible. The three months of classroom theory that had preceded this placement had focused only on textbook 'normal': healthy women at full term with uncomplicated labours – in fact anything but the usual, as would quickly become clear.

My heart pounded in my chest as the list went on, each patient more complex than the last: 'Recovery, para three, post emergency section, 1.4 litre blood loss.' 'High dependency, para nought plus two, twins, day four, sepsis.' 'Room thirteen, stillbirth at twenty-eight weeks.'

Was everyone in this hospital pathological? Did anyone actually come in, labour in a straightforward way for a few hours and push a baby out of their vagina without losing half their circulating blood volume or mainlining an industrial amount of drugs, or both? As the litany of obstructed labours and complications continued, I imagined myself walking back through the car park and driving home, where my husband would be getting my girls out of their baths, bouncy dark curls plastered to their cheeks, their skin soft and soap-smelling. I could stop this all now, I could tell them I had had a change of heart and they would still love me, just excited to have their mum home for bedtime.

'And you are …?' It took a moment to realise that the sister was talking to me. She peered down that impossibly long nose with a withering look that took me in from head to toe: my unfamiliar face, my rictus of naked fear, the ridiculous scrubs and the blindingly new shoes, their gleaming white soles yet to be christened by rainbow trickles of blood and liquor.

'Student midwife,' I squeaked. 'I'm here for six weeks.'

'Nobody told me you were coming. Bloody typical. What year are you?'

'First,' I said. Sister looked pained. This was clearly the wrong answer. She turned towards the whiteboard, scanning it for a patient who could bear the brunt of my hopeless inexperience.

'Room four,' she decided. 'Para one, thirty-nine weeks and six days, spontaneous labour, fully dilated …'

OK, maybe I can handle this, I thought to myself. *A woman who's had one baby already, just a day short of full term, who's got herself into labour and all the way to being fully dilated without any drugs or intervention. With any luck, she'll have delivered before I even get to the room.* Maybe I would stay.

'… and she's got genital warts.'

Ah. The punchline. Sister grinned at me beatifically and looked around the room to see which midwife would be unfortunate enough to be paired with me as my mentor. Her gaze landed on a colleague standing by the door who was as broad as she was tall; almost perfectly square-shaped, with a severe black bob framing her equally angular face and a full sleeve of Maori tattoos trailing down one of her sturdy arms. The smiley-face badge on this midwife's scrub top seemed at odds with her dour expression, which grew even colder when she realised she'd be in charge of me for the night.

'Phyllis,' Sister said to the midwife. 'Take the student.'

Phyllis took a dramatic pause to size me up. She sighed, beckoned to me with a sharp nod and headed down the corridor towards room four without looking back to check whether I was following. Although the temptation to flee was definitely as real as the muffled screams I could hear emanating from every room in the labour ward, some ingrained sense of responsibility (or masochism) propelled me down the corridor. Phyllis chapped the door of room four with quick, sharp blows. Turning to me with the laconic drawl of a jaded general about to lead his hopeless infantry into battle, she said, 'Just do what I tell you.'

I squinted as my eyes adjusted to the scene in front of me; the room was dark but the overhead examination lamp beamed its small, hot pool of light onto the bed. A woman hunched there on all fours, a mane of frizzy golden curls hanging down over her face, her hands white-knuckling the sides of the bed while a steady stream of straw-coloured fluid dripped onto the tangle of green sterile drapes wedged under her knees. At her side, the outgoing day-shift midwife looked up at Phyllis and me with exhausted gratitude, peeling off her gloves with a thwack. I braced myself for the verbal handover I had been taught to expect: a detailed description of the woman's past medical history, her antenatal health, any allergies, her progress in labour and a plan of management. Instead, the midwife said simply, 'She's doing it,' and left the room. I stared blankly at Phyllis, who accepted this pronouncement without question, and I had the creeping realisation that real midwifery bore very little resemblance to any theory I had learned. I was suddenly a foot soldier in an army of warrior women, caught in a campaign whose rules of engagement were beyond my comprehension.

Phyllis and I stood at the end of the bed and surveyed the scene; she with an experienced eye, me with an embarrassed sense that I should be apologising to this stranger for staring at her vulva before we'd even made eye contact.

'Get your gloves on,' ordered Phyllis.

I stared at her dumbly.

'In there,' she said, gesturing to a door, and looked at my hands. 'Six and a halfs, I'm guessing.'

Gloves, gloves, gloves, I chanted to myself, opening the cupboard to be met with an array of unidentifiable packets. What was this long plastic thing? And the whoosit with the wire coming out of it? And who could possibly get through all these sachets of lube? I tossed what was probably several hundred pounds' worth of stock to one side and found a small pile of flat paper packets. I ripped one open and, yes – first success of my midwifery career – I had located gloves. While I congratulated myself, an ear-splitting scream came from over my shoulder.

Phyllis was poised where I'd left her, head so close to this woman's vagina that she could almost have used her nose to push the baby back in again. As it was, a thick strand of viscous red mucus dropped down between the woman's knees, and Phyllis rested her gloved hands on the peach-sized patch of baby's head that was advancing steadily with every contraction. Joining Phyllis at the business end of the bed, I flashed back to my younger self watching the Birth Video in

Mr Katz's classroom. The feeling of wonder was the same, but this view was real and very undeniably in the now – the woman's body a riot of textures and shapes, and in the air the salty, coppery scent of sweaty pennies, of blood, of the sea. More of the head was there, with a fine down of blonde hair slicked by blood and goo, and yes, like a crown of miniature cauliflowers, genital warts covered the woman's distended labia and bloomed in the creases of her groin. This was not how I expected my first birth as a student midwife to look, but it was overwhelming and wild and even beautiful, warts and all.

'Put your hands on the head,' hissed Phyllis. I shook myself out of my trance and slapped my gloves on. 'On the head!' she repeated with clear annoyance.

I placed my hands on the very top of the baby's head, gently flexing it as I had been taught, while keeping a watchful eye on the delicate skin that stretched around it, looking for paper-thin patches that could split into buttonhole tears, or worse. Phyllis placed her hands on mine, guiding me, adjusting the angle of flexion. The woman pushed again.

'Small breaths,' Phyllis called in a gentle, encouraging voice quite different from the one she had used to address me. 'Just breathe it out,' she said, but the surges were too powerful for the woman to control and the baby's head came out in one slippery push, its eyes still closed, its pursed lips blowing mute, mucusy bubbles. In the pause before the next contraction, the baby's head rotated smoothly towards me as its body completed the internal tilts and turns required to pass through the mother's pelvis. It was my textbook in technicolour. It was perfect.

The baby opened its eyes and gazed at me with a cool, level stare. *You are here,* it seemed to be saying. *This is happening.*

Suddenly grounded, calm, I realised that, to some small extent, in my limited capacity, I *did* know what to do. I repositioned my hands, one under the baby's chin and one at the nape of its neck, ready to guide the head and body down and out with the final contraction and, just as I had learned, the last knee-trembling wave sent the baby out in a slick, thrilling rush, first the anterior shoulder, then the posterior, then the body with its tiny arms and legs flailing wildly. My gloves held firm to the baby, Phyllis's hands on my own, as we guided this new human out in one smooth curve. Amniotic fluid splashed onto our forearms as we looped the baby, still attached by its cord, under its mother's legs, helping her to rise up onto her knees with her child clutched to her chest. The woman tossed back her hair and cried loud, racking sobs as her baby made its first tentative squeals. 'Thank God,' she said, gasping, then laughed. 'I thought that would never end.'

Phyllis sprang into a practised routine of efficiency, rubbing the baby briskly with towels, sweeping soiled drapes and pads into bins, boxing instruments and writing notes. I shadowed her clumsily around the room, no doubt more of a hindrance than a help. My mind reeled as my hands flapped at my sides; what I had just seen was too powerful, too monumental to be processed in a moment or two. It was a raw, bloody, towering triumph for this woman, but an everyday occurrence for Phyllis and the rest of the midwives toiling away in this strange factory of new life. As I pointlessly folded and re-folded a pile of blankets that had been warming under the lights of the Resuscitaire, Phyllis nudged my elbow and said, 'The next one's all yours. See one, do one.'

And she was right. As I was to realise over the next three years, midwifery training takes no prisoners:

learning happens quickly, ruthlessly and is quite literally hands-on. The expectation is that you will see your mentor do it once, then do it yourself the next time, whether it's guiding a baby into the world or drawing blood, injecting drugs or scrubbing for an emergency Caesarean section when the baby's heartbeat is in a downward spiral and your own pulse is going a million beats per minute and the phrase 'sick with fear' becomes vividly, sphincter-clenchingly real. Three years and seventy-five births later, after soldiering on through situations that were bloodier and more beautiful than I could ever have imagined, I qualified as a midwife, and my real education began.

Notes on the Women Who 'Shouldn't' be Pregnant

'You shouldn't be pregnant.'

No midwife will ever say this to their patient, but more often than you might believe, there's a midwife who's thinking it. Sometimes the thought is rooted in personal prejudice, plain and simple. Bias and judgement are unavoidable – some might argue, essential – elements of being human, and midwives are hardly exempt from that condition. The drug abuser whose five other children have all been taken into care? There will be a midwife who thinks she shouldn't be pregnant. The morbidly obese woman whose pregnancy is high-risk, whose Caesarean section requires super-human feats of anaesthetic skill and whose postnatal care is dizzyingly complex? There will be a midwife who thinks this is a colossal waste of public funds and clinical efforts.

And the forty-eight-year-old accountant whose green juices, yoga classes and half-marathons keep her in brilliantly rude health? Not even a boatload of kale smoothies could have prevented the multiple miscarriages that drove her to seek IVF abroad, then return to Britain for the safe gestation and delivery of her twins. Many a midwife will sigh and tut over this woman's lengthy case notes, shaking her head as she reads about the expensive trips to the clinic in Madrid and the private scans and the dozen anxious phone calls to Triage for every spot and twinge. Later, in the cosy, windowless confines of the tea room, this midwife will lecture her colleagues at length about these women who 'think it's their God-given right to be pregnant'. Her colleagues will nod mutely as they race against the clock to bolt down mouthfuls of microwave meals; it's a familiar debate, and few have the time or energy to engage. This midwife will then toss back the dregs of her tea, rinse her mug and return to the bedside. She will smile guilelessly as she straps the monitoring belts around her patient's abdomen and she will tell this mother-to-be how wonderful it is that these twins have defied the odds and come into being. She will be kind and she will crack a dirty joke that makes the patient and her husband laugh. She will embrace them both warmly as they leave the unit, and no one but the other staff at the other bedsides will know how she really feels.

I can't speak for every midwife everywhere, and I don't pretend to be devoid of my own irrational preconceptions, but for me, these distinctions between women who 'should' and 'shouldn't' be pregnant are as meaningless as they are unhelpful. Each of us exists only as a unique and infinitely unlikely cosmic coincidence: would you be here if your father hadn't caught a whiff of your mother's perfume one afternoon on the number 66 bus or if your grandparents hadn't kept trying for a baby even after twelve years of wishful failure or if your great-great-great-grandmother hadn't fled her home country to seek safety in the land where your great-great-great-grandfather lived and was lonely, desperate for a bride? To question the worth or wisdom of any pregnancy is inherently hypocritical, but for a midwife, it's a particularly moot point. By the very nature of our job, by the time we meet a woman, she is pregnant, she is in our care. The deed is done; now keep her safe.

Eleanor:
Defying the Odds

Eleanor was one in a trillion: a human anomaly, a pregnant fluke, a walking, gestating embodiment of improbability. As I prepared a room for her in the labour suite at the start of one night shift, I had no idea that I was creating the backdrop for a scene that would defy every possible law of luck and nature.

The sister in charge had simply barked, 'Set up a room': the command that precedes every labourer's arrival, from the bright-eyed primigravida to the world-weary para four. To the patient, the room is a blank slate: you see the bed with its starched sheets, the wipe-clean chair, the cot with its teddy-bear flannelette. Each item appears freshly minted, placed there just for you by an unseen yet benevolent hand. To me, the empty room is already crowded with the ghosts of all the women I have ever looked after in that space; the babies I have rubbed frantically with towels at the Resuscitaire, willing them to cry; the splashes of blood

I have wiped off the floors; the dip and weave of all the fetal heartbeats I have listened to in the wee small hours, crossing my fingers and chewing my lips with worry. *What will it be this time?* I wondered as I drifted into room two, where the floors were still wet from the auxiliary's mop.

This particular night's patient was still a mystery to me, but the routine of setting up was comfortingly familiar: first, arrange my stack of paperwork in a neat pile on the worktop next to two white name bands that would go around the baby's ankles. Check the Resuscitaire: flick on the overhead lamp, placing a bundle of soft blankets and towels beneath it to warm. Check the pressure in the oxygen, in the suction; flinch as the air cylinders shriek when I turn their valves. A tiny nappy to the side, a plastic clamp for the baby's cord; a pink hat, a blue hat and a lemon-yellow hat with a jaunty orange stripe running through it, all knitted by the anonymous grannies who provide us with a steady supply of bonnets and cardigans. I moved around the room, plumping pillows on the bed, switching on the monitors, opening the cupboards to make sure that every possible item I might need in the next twelve-and-a-quarter hours was present and correct: gloves, jelly, a selection of needles of different bores and gauges, catheters, cannulas, IV fluids, fetal scalp electrodes, the aptly but terrifyingly named Amnihook; all the tools of my trade were there, from the basic to the brutal.

There was a brisk knock at the door and I opened it to find Fatima, a midwife from the antenatal ward, bearing a thick sheaf of case notes.

'Hey, Fatima,' I said. I looked over her shoulder. 'Where's the patient?'

She laid the case notes down on the worktop and nodded towards the corridor. 'You'll have a good night. They're *lesbians,*' she whispered, 'but they're lovely.' I laughed inwardly – should it be a surprise or an exception for lesbians to be lovely? – but I was glad of the glowing report. This informal part of the midwife's handover is just as important as the summary of the patient's clinical history: your hopes for a shift can live or die by an optimistic, 'She'll do great,' or a dry, 'Good luck with this one.' I craned my neck to peer further along the corridor and heard peals of laughter before I saw Eleanor waddling towards me. She had glossy dark hair, a scattering of freckles over a golden-brown tan and a perfectly round bump straining beneath a black-and-white striped top. Everything about her overall appearance and the slow, easy roll of her hips suggested vibrant good health and the intangible energy of a woman on the precipice of labour. As she finally reached the door, she pretended to collapse against the frame.

'Right, that's it,' she said, panting in mock exhaustion, hand on hip. 'I'm knackered. You'll just need to press "eject" and get this baby out for me, I've got nothing left.'

I smiled and winked at Fatima as she left the room. 'I've been looking for that eject button for years and I still haven't found it,' I quipped. I went to close the door behind her, then stopped. 'Is there anybody here with you?'

'She's just coming,' she replied. 'She's a wee bit tired.'

I was about to say, 'My heart bleeds for her' – the standard midwifey riposte for the birth partner, male or female, who claims to be suffering from pains, cramps or niggles while the mother-to-be is tied up in knots with gut-clenching contractions. Anyone who is unfortunate enough to admit that he or she faints at the sight of blood is met with an even less forgiving reply: 'If you pass out, we'll just step over you.' However, when I saw the gaunt figure lurching up the corridor, every snappy comeback faltered on my tongue. Where Eleanor was the archetypal picture of a glowing pregnant woman, her partner, Liz, brought tangible meaning to the phrase 'a shadow of herself'. Her skin was so pale as to be almost translucent, eyes edged with violet smudges of fatigue, her body stiff and frail. She had obviously made an effort to look smart for the occasion – crisp white shirt, indigo jeans and buttery suede loafers – but she looked more like a gangly teenager dressed up in her big sister's clothes, an effect heightened by the blue knitted beanie hat pulled down over her ears. Liz's shuffling gait finally brought her to the room, where she paused, sighed deeply and braced a skeletal hand against the door.

'Where's the baby?' she said. 'I gave you enough bloody time getting up that corridor, I thought you'd have given birth by now.'

Eleanor held Liz's face in her hands and squeezed her cheeks playfully. 'You big daftie,' she said, laughing. 'I've had twins – they're away home in a taxi.'

Liz smiled and kissed her wife. 'What a woman,' she said weakly.

I already felt as though I were interrupting something; whatever had happened to Liz, it had obviously only served to bring her and Eleanor closer. Every couple that come to the labour ward bring their own dynamic: some are already fractious and tense, any cracks in the relationship magnified by nine tumultuous months of pregnancy, while others, like Liz and Eleanor, present an intimacy that's wonderful to behold, but which is virtually impenetrable to even the wiliest midwife's best efforts. Nevertheless, a good birth can sometimes hinge on the partnership and trust between a woman and her midwife, and a good midwife is skilled in establishing a rapport as quickly and effectively as time permits. *This will be interesting*, I thought, as Eleanor and Liz entered the room, their movements mirroring each other with the subtle twinning of the most harmonious couples.

'Welcome to Labour Ward,' I began, gesturing to the room around us. 'This is where the magic happens. Go ahead and make yourselves at home while I have a quick read of your paperwork.' Liz flopped into the pale green easy chair in the corner of the room while Eleanor rifled through bags for a nightie and I began to leaf through her notes, scanning the pages for any clue to Liz's condition. So far, so normal. Eleanor was a flight attendant, Liz was a pilot; it was Eleanor's first pregnancy, using donor sperm and Liz's egg, but that in itself was unremarkable in a time when assisted conception has become almost commonplace. Over the course of my training, I'd become accustomed to caring for women whose babies were conceived in labs in every corner of Europe; every combination you can imagine of donor and surrogate egg, sperm and womb – I had seen it. Gone were the days when 'test-tube babies' or same-sex couples (or both at once) raised any eyebrows in a hospital seeing many thousands of births a year and getting busier all the time.

I kept reading, flipping through sheets of routine scans and blood tests, while Eleanor shimmied into a hot-pink nightgown and Liz shifted gently in her chair. Then, in a typed letter from the consultant to the GP, tucked away at the back of the folder, I found what I was looking for:

Eleanor underwent three cycles of IVF using her wife Liz's eggs and donor sperm from Denmark. The final cycle has, happily, resulted in a continuing pregnancy. However, Eleanor tells me that two weeks

> *after conception, Liz was diagnosed with breast*
> *cancer and is likely to require surgery and chemo-*
> *therapy during the course of her wife's pregnancy.*

I looked up from the notes. Eleanor was toying with the stirrups on the end of the bed and leaned over to whisper something in her wife's ear, cackling filthily while a blush temporarily illuminated Liz's wan face. Not only would it be difficult for me to work my way into their cosy circle of two, but they were going through an ordeal of which I had no experience. At this time, my life was remarkably untouched by cancer and although I had seen friends and colleagues grapple with its horror, the illness was something that I could then only pretend to understand.

I cleared my throat, and ventured, 'You've had quite a time of it.' They both looked over; they seemed to have forgotten that I was in the room and were still smiling sheepishly at whatever private joke had passed between them. I was aware of my voice's false, brittle brightness echoing around the room; nevertheless, I continued. 'So, how are things now?'

'Things are really good,' Eleanor said, her eyes still on Liz. 'Liz had a double mastectomy and she's had four cycles of chemo so far. She's still got a few more to go, but she's been an absolute star.'

'That's amazing,' I replied, painfully aware of the insufficiency of my words. And then, to Liz, 'How are you feeling?'

She leaned back in the chair. 'It's …' She sighed and looked at Eleanor. 'It's complicated, as they say. Obviously, I'm so excited about the baby and the doctors say there's a decent chance that I'll be cancer-free in the long term, so that's the main thing, but … I'm tired. It's like the worst jet lag ever, and I mean, I've had some jet lag in my time.'

'You're a pilot?'

'Well, I was, I mean, I am, but I've been grounded by this whole thing.' She smiled grimly. 'Cancer is a no-fly zone, apparently. And it's shit for your hair.' She lifted a corner of the beanie hat to reveal the smooth baldness underneath and, as she did so, I realised that her neatly arched eyebrows had been stencilled on with painstaking precision. I wasn't sure whether to smile, laugh, commiserate or all three. I couldn't pretend to understand what she'd been through; all I knew was that this night was only one of many staging points on a long, hard journey. The best I could do was to infuse our brief time together with a little love; not the romantic kind, but the kind that every midwife magics up for new parents whom she may never have met before. It was an instant, automatic love that I was used to giving unsparingly, and these two women were welcome to their share.

Eleanor was sitting on the edge of the bed, listening intently to Liz. She reached over to squeeze her wife's hand. 'Liz might need a bit of a disco nap at some point,' she said. 'It's been a while since we pulled an all-nighter.' She winked at Liz and Liz smiled again, weakly this time.

'Disco naps are no problem,' I reassured her. 'Eleanor and I are in the Wide Awake Club, but you chill when you need to. Sit back, relax.' I nodded to the radio, which was thrumming gently with some late-night reggae. 'Enjoy the beats.'

As Eleanor and Liz settled in, murmuring softly to each other under the music and drawing their cloak of intimacy back around them, I began to make the familiar preparations for this final stage of induction of labour. In many hospitals, induction is a standard approach to childbirth for women who've conceived via IVF; this practice hangs by a slender thread of evidence, but as is so often the case in our increasingly litigious culture when there is even a whiff of risk, it has become the norm. *2x hormone pessaries given and cervix now 3cm dilated,* Fatima's most recent notes declared in bold, looping script. *Fine*, I thought; protocol dictated that I would next break Eleanor's waters, to bring the baby's head into direct contact with the cervix, encouraging stronger contractions. For women who have already had a baby, this is often enough to tip the body into full-blown labour, but for first-time mothers, a slow drip of synthetic hormones is usually also needed to kick-start the uterus. Just as a chef would gather all the ingredients and utensils required to bake an elaborate cake, so I began to set out the instruments and medicines that would be required to encourage Eleanor's baby into the world. I laid an examination pack, gloves, jelly and an Amni-hook on the wheeled metal trolley by the bedside before turning my attention to the drip. I opened a tiny glass ampoule of Syntocinon with a satisfying snap, then drew up its contents and injected them into a large bag of clear fluids that would be run through an electronic pump at a carefully modulated rate, ratcheted up in half-hourly increments until Eleanor was in the throes of labour. Just one millilitre of this hormone – sometimes referred to as 'the good stuff' or even 'jungle juice' by the more jaded among us – was enough to move mountains.

'If it's OK with you, Eleanor, I'd like to do a baseline examination now and break your waters,' I said, concealing the Amnihook with careful tact behind the other packets on the trolley. 'You'll feel lots of cold jelly and some pressure, but it shouldn't hurt. If it becomes too much for you at any time, tell me and I'll stop straight away.'

Eleanor grimaced and began to hoick up her nightie. 'Usually I would at least get taken out for dinner and drinks before this kind of carry-on. I've never had so many fingers up my fanny in my life.'

Liz raised a neat eyebrow and chuckled to herself.

'Never mind,' Eleanor said as she opened her legs. 'Wire in.'

I washed my hands, gloved up and did what was needed, sliding the Amnihook in towards the bag of waters and tugging gently at its membrane until I felt the familiar pop. A stream of fluid begin to run in clear rivers onto the paper mats I'd pre-emptively wedged under Eleanor's bottom. I bundled up the sodden pads and replaced them with fresh ones, which were soaked as soon as I laid them down. Two more pad changes later and the warm flow had slowed to a trickle. 'Job done,' I said, smiling, as I pulled a fresh sheet up over Eleanor's legs. 'Your waters have gone and the drip is up. We've reached cruising altitude.'

All was serene. Eleanor tied her hair up into a loose ponytail, smoothed down the front of her nightie and relaxed back onto the pillows of the bed. Liz slipped off her loafers and slung herself sideways in the chair, her feet dangling over one side. The CTG monitor drummed reassuringly; the baby who would never have existed without the many wonders of modern science was letting us know that all was well in spite of its watery pool being suddenly drained. *22.00*, I wrote in Eleanor's notes. *Patient is resting comfortably, fetal heartbeat 128 beats per minute, uterine activity mild and crampy, clear liquor draining.*

Eleanor closed her eyes and shifted on the bed. I could see the first shadows of discomfort playing across her brow, but she breathed deeply and was able to sigh them away. 'You must be so bored,' she said, eyes still shut. 'Don't you want to take a break?'

I waited for Liz to respond, but her eyes were also closed.

'Who, me?' I said.

'Yes, you … it must be so tedious just watching women lie there, waiting for something to happen. I mean, I'm totally fine.' She grimaced, shifted again, and opened her eyes. 'I feel terrible making you wait. Don't you want to get a coffee or read a magazine? I've got a few in my bag.' She prodded Liz, who was deep into her first snooze. 'Lizzie! Get the midwife those magazines – they're in the side pocket of the blue case.'

I laughed at Eleanor, ever the accommodating flight attendant, trying to look after me and keep me comfortable even as the roles were reversed. I could imagine her striding down the aisle of a 737 with her trolley of drinks and snacks, winking and twinkling and playing to her adoring audience as she tonged ice cubes into plastic cups of vodka and Coke. It was harder to imagine Liz in the cockpit, quietly confident at the controls, sharp-eyed, healthy.

'Please don't worry,' I said. 'I'm pretty sure you'll be keeping me entertained.'

It's a strange thing, watching someone cross over into the shady world of pain, and it's an even stranger thing to find yourself willing them to make that journey. As a midwife, you know that it's possible to be 'far too comfortable'. It is your role to chaperone your patient into Labourland, giving her the odd nudge and budge, sometimes watching her rush on ahead of you, sometimes taking her by the hand and pulling her deeper into unknown territory if she straggles or strays behind. You want your patient to be niggly, to be sore, to hurt and yet, at the same time, you are desperate to give her solace, to show her that she is loved and safe. I watched as Eleanor did the familiar dance of the early labourer; she moved her weight from one side to the other on the bed, then perched on the edge of the mattress, then heaved herself over onto all fours with a groan as the drip began to work its wonders on her uterus.

Patient becoming uncomfortable with uterine activity now moderate, 3 in 10 minutes, lasting 45–60 seconds. FH 142 bpm. Syntocinon IV runs at 36 mls per hour, I wrote, then smiled as I put my pen down. You may think this was cruel, but I knew that the quicker Eleanor embarked on her voyage across labour's stormy seas, the quicker she would reach her destination.

The sound of Eleanor's pain must have reached Liz even in the depths of her fatigue; her eyes flashed open and she looked around in panic at her wife, and at her surroundings, until she realised where she was and what was happening. Leaning in to Eleanor, whose face was burrowed in the pile of pillows on the bed, she asked, 'You OK, babe?'

'I want an epidural,' came the muffled reply. With a massive effort, Eleanor reared back onto her knees, then heaved herself round so that she was sitting up in the bed once again. Strands of her hair were plastered against her forehead and her cheeks were flushed beneath their freckled tan. 'If I get an epidural, will I still have to feel pain?'

'Well,' I said, 'it's useful to be able to feel something down below when you get to the pushing stage of your labour, but we can try to tweak the dose to give you some sensation when the time comes. With a really effective epidural, you won't feel anything from the waist down.'

'No change there then,' Eleanor drawled, looking sideways at Liz, who gasped in mock outrage, and Eleanor threw her head back, unleashing another throaty laugh. This time, Liz joined in, chuckling with a delight that was free, easy and a joy to behold. Fatima was right, I thought. We'll have a good night.

And so it went. Another midwife came to relieve me for my first short break of the shift and by the time I'd bolted down a slice of banana loaf and a cup of strong, muddy coffee and returned to the room, the anaesthetist had been and gone. The monitor was picking up much stronger contractions now, about four in every ten minutes, and the epidural was running through its own little pump at the bedside, pushing a small but powerful trickle of anaesthetic into a tiny space in Eleanor's spine. Eleanor looked relaxed, and as the muscles in her face softened, so Liz also settled back into the chair, tucking her feet beneath her. The clock on the wall had just clicked past midnight. It was this baby's birthday.

I rolled a big pink birth ball out of its hiding place in the adjoining stockroom and placed it by the bedside, where I could comfortably bounce the hours away while the jungle juice did its thing. Eleanor's epidural was flawlessly effective; I placed a hand gently on her abdomen and could feel taut waves of pressure rolling across her bump, but she was none the wiser, snoring gently, slack-jawed, as a glassy bead of saliva slid down her chin. In a way, she had been right:

watching women sleep can be simultaneously tedious and challenging, especially when you are duty-bound to stay awake and alert for the slightest glitch in the baby's heartbeat. My coping strategies for this particular challenge are two-fold: first of all, the aforementioned coffee. Secondly, I break my night into fifteen-minute intervals. In fifteen minutes, I think, I will document the fetal heartbeat. In another fifteen minutes, I will check the patient's 'pressure areas' – her knees, her hips, and so on – and document this action by ticking the relevant boxes on the 'Skin Surveillance' form, one of the many gaily coloured but undeniably onerous pieces of paperwork required in our hospital during the care of a labouring woman. Fifteen minutes after that, I will rearrange the packs in the top left-hand cupboard by order of size and then arrange the needles by colour, and then shuffle them all and start again.

It was 05.47 when the baby's pulse, which had been sitting squarely in the 'safe zone' of between 110 and 160 beats per minute, began to edge its way downwards. I had been sliding slowly off the birth ball as exhaustion set in, but when I heard that warning skip and lurch in between beats, I sat upright, the ball squeaking beneath me. *Fetal heart 95 bpm.* OK, it was coming up again. Slowly, but coming up. *Good recovery to baseline,* I wrote. *Observing carefully.* I ran my hands through my hair and gave myself a bit of a slap around the chops. (Did I mention that a bit of light masochism is Coping Strategy Number Three?) Eleanor and Liz were still sleeping and the first glow of sunrise was beginning to illuminate the frosted-glass window at the back of Liz's chair. Boom. Boom boom. Boom. *86 beats per minute.* I stood up and the ball rolled silently away across the floor. Boom. *82 beats per minute.* Here we go. I could hear somebody screaming in one of the other labour rooms. Too bad. I lunged towards the emergency buzzer – and pulled it.

'Eleanor,' I called, shaking her shoulder. She opened her eyes woozily and rubbed her nose with the back of her hand. Itchy nose: a little-known side effect of epidurals and the least of Eleanor's problems at that moment. 'Eleanor, I need you to try to roll onto your left side. It's a better position for getting oxygenated blood to the baby. I'll help you.'

Turning Eleanor was easier said than done as the epidural had made her more or less a dead weight from the waist down and her legs swung heavily from her hips as I hauled her over. Just as I managed to roll her onto her side, the door opened and Caroline, the labour suite sister for the night, came to the bedside.

'What do we have here?' she said as she looked from Eleanor to me to the monitor. And then, sharply, 'I'll get the reg.' Before she had even turned around, Missy, the night's registrar, was there. A strikingly tall woman with cropped peroxide hair and an earful of silver studs and bars, Missy was hardly the standard-bearer for the NHS uniform policy, but her piercings had – funnily enough – never interfered with her clinical judgement. *Dr Walker present for review*, I wrote with relief. Sitting alone in a room with a dodgy CTG is a very lonely thing; it was good to have backup.

'Eleanor, I'm Missy, the doctor on call tonight,' said the registrar, barely taking her eyes from the numbers on the monitor's screen. 'I'm going to examine you. We need to know whether you're about to deliver vaginally or whether we need to take you to theatre.' Liz, who had just awoken to find the room full of strangers, looked at Eleanor with undisguised terror. Eleanor, in turn, looked pleadingly at me, searching my face for clues or reassurance. I felt her distress keenly but was also preoccupied with finding the right gloves and packs for Missy; there was no time for light banter or, for that matter, any hesitation whatsoever.

Missy sat side-saddle on the bed, eyes narrowed and fixed on an invisible point on the wall as her fingers probed under Eleanor's sheet.

'You're fully dilated,' she said tersely to Eleanor, and then, to me, 'Vertex at spines plus two.' The baby's head was well down in the pelvis. 'Set up for a ventouse. We should be able to do this in the room, but if not, we'll head to theatre for a trial of forceps.'

'She's going to use a suction cup,' I explained to Eleanor as I heaved her feet into the stirrups she'd been playing with a few hours before. 'The doctor will pull, but you'll still need to push.' There wasn't time to say much more. Caroline had wheeled in one of the emergency trolleys with the ventouse and its accoutrements. Missy was gloving up in the corner. A paediatrician (or 'paed', as they are often called) had been paged and was hanging back by the Resuscitaire; a baby with a non-reassuring trace can surprise everyone by coming out crying or it can confirm its hours of compromise by sliding out slack-limbed and unresponsive, requiring urgent intervention that can range from a few puffs of oxygen to intubation and full-on life support. The paed remained in the shadows, waiting, poised for disaster.

Meanwhile, I hunched over Eleanor's feet, flames of pain licking down my back as I unclipped the entire bottom of the bed from its hinges and heaved it onto the floor, leaving Eleanor in a kind of stirruped throne that would allow the doctor to get right in between her legs. I grimaced as my spine burned, but my body's labour was insignificant in that moment; there would be time for rest and relief when this job was done.

Beat. Beat beat. This baby needed to come, this baby whose existence defied the laws of science, this baby with a far-away father and two adoring mothers, one of whom, at another time, might not be alive – this baby that was hovering in the hazy limbo between one world and the next. We were all willing it to make that last leap through impossibility, to squeeze through those few remaining millimetres and greet us with a cry. Missy was on a stool between Eleanor's legs; she reached in and applied the ventouse cup to the baby's head, a sliver of which had slid into view with the last contraction. *06.03,* I scribbled. *Vertex visible. Ventouse applied.* 'When the next one comes,' Missy commanded, 'push hard.'

I stood at Eleanor's side, my hand on her abdomen so that I could tell her when her next contraction was beginning. Her epidural block was still dense; she had none of the ferocious, involuntary urge to push that women often have at this stage. As I felt the familiar tension building at the top of Eleanor's bump, like a balloon being inflated in one slow, steady breath beneath my fingertips, I turned to her, locking her eyes to mine and said simply, 'Now.'

Eleanor tucked her chin down onto her chest, drew a deep breath and pushed as long and hard as she could, squeezing the rumpled sheets with one hand and Liz's skinny wrist with the other. As her breath became ragged, she opened her eyes and looked hopefully across her bump at Missy. 'Anything?'

'Slowly,' Missy said, her eyes still fixed between Eleanor's legs. With every push, Missy would need to give an equal pull. 'Go again.'

The hormone drip was running at 60 millilitres per hour, its highest safe level, and as it pulsed into Eleanor's veins, a mighty surge rolled through her abdomen. 'Again, Eleanor!' I called to her. Her eyes were closed once more, and she pushed. There was silence in the room; a still fissure in time.

And then came a gurgle, like a spring bubbling up suddenly from the soil, and then a gasp and then a cry. In a slippery flash of pink, with hardly a pause between head, shoulders and body, the baby rocketed out into Missy's hands, and then into mine. I passed this wet, screaming thing onto Eleanor's chest, and the paed started rubbing it with a warm towel, and Caroline was laughing, and Eleanor and Liz were looking at each other, crying, aghast, amazed. I lifted an edge of the towel and then one of the baby's tiny, wrinkle-toed feet. 'It's a boy,' I said. 'Happy birthday, baby.' *06.07,* I noted silently. *Ventouse delivery of live male infant, cried at birth.*

Eleanor broke her gaze from Liz and looked down at their boy, seeing him for the first time, taking in every inch of his slick, fat little body: his shoulders, daubed with vernix; his downy blonde hair, still wet with streaks of liquor that smelled of rock pools and bracken. This was the woman who should never have been pregnant, whose love was still named in whispers, whose wife was a walking miracle of modern medicine, whose baby was a dazzling feat of reproductive science. Eleanor kissed the top of her baby boy's head, and she smiled.

Notes on Children Having Children

'Lock her up. It's the only contraception you can trust'.

This was the advice ruefully given to me by Bridget, a woman whose fifteen-year-old daughter, Shannon, had just arrived at the hospital in early labour. I knelt by the bed and watched Shannon writhe with the fresh horror of each contraction as it rippled through her size-zero frame, every surge seeming to catch her by surprise. *Could this one possibly hurt as much as the last?* her face seemed to say. *Will it ever stop?* Yes, was the answer. And also, blessedly, yes. Her labour was fast, as often seems to be the case for the youngest mothers, and two hours later she gave birth to her own little girl, clutching Bridget's hand the whole time and crying for her mum even as the baby latched onto her breast.

Many reports in recent years have highlighted the increasing number of older women having babies: 'elderly primigravidas', as medics cruelly used to call them, conjuring images of fetuses springing forth from dusty, wrinkled wombs. Although there's no denying that the average age of the pregnant population is climbing slowly skywards, there are also still thousands of women giving birth every year who are, well, children. Some, like Shannon, conceive after only their second or third fumbling attempt at sex. Others, Shannon's age or younger, make up a small but growing group whose bulging bellies are the by-products of trafficking and abuse.

Whatever the context, looking after such young women has always struck me as a unique challenge. On the one hand, as the mother of two girls, teenagers send my protective impulses into overdrive and my urge to shield them from pain, upset and the multiple cruelties that the world inflicts on women becomes almost irrationally strong, even if some of these girls are already more streetwise and battle-hardened than I will ever be. On the other hand, the very examinations and procedures that I need to perform in order to do my job can become deeply uncomfortable where young girls are involved. How do you explain a vaginal examination to a fourteen-year-old who's never had a smear test or more than a handful of periods, and who's certainly never been touched 'down there' by someone she could trust? Does it feel right to inject pain-relieving diamorphine – which, to be blunt, is simply medical-grade heroin – into the skinny thigh of a teenager whose body is the same size and shape as your child's, even if she's begging and screaming for you to 'just give me the jag already'? When children have children, the midwife needs to ask herself a hundred tricky questions and, even after countless Shannons, there are no easy answers.

Crystal: Twenty-three Weeks and Three Days

I was in the middle of writing myself a thank-you card when Crystal arrived on the ward. Lest you think I'm some kind of egomaniac who needs to write herself a congratulatory note every time she empties a bedpan, please allow me to explain.

I was sitting by the bedside of Mrs Bhatti, a Bangladeshi woman who was thirty-seven weeks pregnant with her fifth child, and who was about to be discharged from the ward following a two-week admission with a kidney infection. Although I was just filling a staff shortfall that day and had never met this particular patient before that morning's handover, I was lucky enough to bear the full force of her gratitude. She was packing up when I drew back her curtain, attempting to fit fourteen days' worth of pyjamas, toiletries and assorted packs of fragrant snacks into a large zebra-print suitcase. Wearing a lime-green Adidas hoodie over a brilliant orange shalwar kameez, Mrs Bhatti almost appeared to glow as she moved around the bed, an effect which was only heightened when she turned to greet me with a broad, gap-toothed smile.

'Good morning, dear,' she said, clutching one of my hands with both of hers. Her grip was surprisingly strong, her hands warm and dry around mine. 'You help me now,' she commanded brightly.

'I'd love to help you, Mrs Bhatti,' I said, 'but I actually just need to give you your discharge paperwork, and then you can go home to your family. Is somebody coming to collect you?'

She drew close to me and put her palms on my cheeks, her eyebrows furrowing into a solid black line as the smile fell from her face. 'You help me now,' she repeated, more urgently this time.

I laughed nervously, wondering what kind of assistance this woman could need so desperately. Was she still in pain? Or in their keen focus on treating her illness, had the ward staff overlooked some kind of terrible personal predicament? I began to do a mental inventory of the many and varied disasters that women had disclosed to me over the years during hushed bedside chats such as this, before Mrs Bhatti's vice-like grip on my chin brought me back into the moment.

'You help me now.'

'Yes,' I intoned, bracing myself stoically for whatever chilling secrets she might be about to share. 'I will help you now. Tell me what you need, Mrs Bhatti.'

'You write thank-you card,' she said. Her face creased back into that brilliant smile, and she released me, clapping her hands with delight and chuckling mischievously as I blushed at my misguided concern. She didn't need saving; she'd seen the earnest do-gooder in me and called my bluff to great effect.

'Ooooh,' I said, laughing breezily as if I'd been in on the joke all along. 'Of course. Yes. I'll help you write a card. Who is it for?'

Mrs Bhatti rummaged through a pile of magazines at the foot of the bed and brought forth a card with a cartoonish picture of two ducks hugging on the front, their wings wrapped tightly around each other, tiny red love hearts dancing above their beaks. She passed me the card, opened it and pointed to the inscription: *Quack you very much.* 'It is a card for staff,' she said. 'For you.'

'For me? But I'm only working here today to cover a staff shortage. All the other midwives have been looking after you for two weeks. It's very kind, but ...' Mrs Bhatti's hand clasped my shoulder and pressed me down into the chair at her bedside in one swift motion. At five foot nothing, she hardly towered over me, but her presence was powerful.

'You write the card, dear. You say thank you.'

'You want me to write a thank-you card ... to me?'

'My English is not good, dear. What shall we say? You write now,' she said, and pointed again to the card, and then to the selection of pens in my tunic pocket.

So I sat dutifully with a pen poised in mid-air, searching for the words that would adequately express my overwhelming gratitude to myself. Mrs Bhatti grinned and nodded her approval as I put pen to paper.

'Dear Leah,' I said out loud as I wrote, 'thank you so much for all of your hard work,' and sensing that she was expecting a little more than a casual one-liner, I drew a smiley face, a love heart, and three kisses below. I tucked the card into its envelope and passed it to Mrs Bhatti, who then passed it back to me and gestured for me to open it. To complete the panto-mime, I slipped open the envelope as if I had no idea of its contents, took an appropriate amount of time to read the inscription and tried to look suitably surprised, touched and humbled.

'Thank you, Mrs Bhatti.'

'Thank *you*, dear.'

'Thanks so much.'

'Thank you, dear.'

She put her arms around me and drew me in to her soft little body and, in return, I patted her gently between the small, bony wings of her shoulder blades, the way one might comfort an elderly aunt who couldn't remember where she'd put her specs. As she squeezed me even tighter, I relaxed into her embrace, morning sunshine spilling over us from her bedside window. I felt that I could quite happily stay there for the rest of my shift, thanking and being thanked, breathing in the warm, sweet scent of Mrs Bhatti's hair.

'All right, Mother Teresa, you've got an admission.'

June, the other midwife on the ward that day, had drawn back the curtain and was now surveying our cosy embrace with undisguised irritation, jaw clenched like a sharp-shooting sheriff in an obstetrically themed spaghetti western. Cuddling a patient? Please. To the most hardened of midwives, walking in on such an emotive scene is far more distasteful than wading through the stream of bodily fluids that winds through our daily work. These world-weary battleaxes have grown a tough, calloused skin during their many hard-fought years of professional practice and, as I was soon to learn, there was a certain wisdom in that grim adaptation. Under June's withering gaze, I was nothing but a soft-hearted fool, ill-equipped for the demands of the job.

'Room six, bed two,' June droned as I pocketed my thank-you card, disentangled myself from Mrs Bhatti, and followed her down the corridor. 'Crystal, a fifteen-year-old PPROM at twenty-three and three, with Mickey Mouse pyjamas and the face of an eight-year-old. Good luck.' June shuffled back to her own patients on the other side of the ward as I hovered by the door to room six.

A PPROM – or preterm, prelabour rupture of membranes – is when the protective bag of fluid around a baby starts leaking before thirty-seven weeks (the widely accepted minimum gestation of a fully grown fetus), and well before the onset of labour. Sometimes women with this condition can safely continue their pregnancy for days, or even weeks, with the support of oral antibiotics and regular check-ups. For others, a PPROM can escalate rapidly into a full-on gush of waters, the start of strong, regular contractions and the birth of a baby whose bird-like body, immature lungs and delicate immune system are immensely vulnerable. This situation is even more precarious around twenty-four weeks of pregnancy. Until fairly recently, the majority of babies born prior to this point died soon after birth or succumbed to serious illness in the weeks that followed. As a consequence, most babies born up to this gestational age were not actively resuscitated and were officially classified as a late miscarriage rather than a registrable birth, as callous as that may feel to those who have experienced the sorrow of losing an extremely preterm child. The chances of survival into infancy and beyond have always tended to increase incrementally with every week that passes *in utero*. Accordingly, any babies born after twenty-four weeks have traditionally been deemed 'viable' by British law and have therefore been offered the full catalogue of cutting-edge paediatric treatment, even if that means intubation, ventilation and weeks of uncomfortable but potentially life-saving procedures in the short term, and a myriad of potential disabilities and developmental delays in the long term.

Regardless of one's personal beliefs about the definition of viability and the value of an early life, doctors who hover over this moral knife edge on a daily basis need to rely on hard-and-fast guidelines to create treatment plans with the best possible chance of a decent outcome. As modern neonatology developed, the twenty-four-week boundary provided medical staff with a clear sense of what could and should be done for babies born too soon, but recent advances in the field have improved survival rates for extremely preterm babies, blurring the line of viability. In spite of the risks of long-term disability, more and more babies born in the increasingly grey zone of twenty-three to twenty-four weeks have been successfully resuscitated and kept alive, defying these tiny creatures' frailty and their inability to breathe, suck or do very much of anything without major intervention. At twenty-three weeks and three days, Crystal's baby was right in the middle of this no-man's land and, if it were born, its survival would depend not only on its own meagre strength, but also on the extremely subjective judgement of the paediatric team on that given day. To make matters even more complex – if such a thing were possible – any decisions Crystal made would be subject to more than the usual amount of scrutiny by the medical team, given that she was legally, if not physically, still a child herself.

I heard Crystal before I saw her. Her curtain was drawn, but she appeared to be having an animated conversation with somebody at her bedside.

'So I said that her pal's cousin was a fucking liar, because I saw her up the shops with Danny's brother last week and she looked like a pure clown, like a fucking riot.'

I pulled the curtain back just enough to see the end of the bed, where Crystal was wiggling her feet back and forth in a pair of pink fluffy slippers. I could see a flash of ankle, and yes, the hem of Mickey Mouse pyjama bottoms. Crystal laughed loudly and, as I drew closer, I saw that she was lying back on a pile of pillows, phone propped up on her knees, FaceTiming a friend who was visible only on the tiny screen of her mobile phone.

'She's all sugar or all shite, that Britney,' said Crystal, sighing. Then, catching sight of me, she sat up in bed and brought the phone back up towards her ear. The phone cover was a giant latex panda with googly eyes. 'Right, I need to go, the nurse is here. Right, right, OK, bye, bye, see you later.' Then, to me, 'Hiya.' She beamed and her smile was a gleaming, crowded jumble, a few tiny milk teeth still vying for space with their permanent cousins – an orthodontist's dream.

The face of an eight-year-old may have been a bit of an exaggeration, but not a million miles from the truth. Crystal looked barely old enough to be in secondary school, let alone in the hospital on her own and on the brink of having a preterm delivery. Even in her current condition, I couldn't imagine her thinking that boys were anything other than gross – in fact, maybe the escapades that brought her to hospital had only reinforced that opinion. She had evidently tried to contour her cheeks in line with the latest make-up trend, but the stripes of bronzer across her face made her look like a child who'd fallen asleep in a bowl of Coco Pops. Something about this misguided attempt at glamour reminded me of my teenage self, although Crystal exuded a kind of easy charisma that I could only have dreamed of at that age. She was a young girl trying on the identity of a ballsy, brazen woman, and the effect was both awkward and compelling.

I wheeled a blood-pressure machine up to the bedside and started with the classic opening line of midwives, nurses and doctors everywhere: 'So tell me what's been happening.' Strangely, this greeting brings me out in a cold sweat when uttered by my own GP, who's about as threatening as a box of kittens. My hands shake, my voice quivers and the cool, collected midwife suddenly becomes a stammering mess, unable even to request a repeat prescription without apologising at least twelve times for wasting the doctor's time. Put me in a blue tunic and a pair of beaten-up orthopaedic shoes, though, and I'm back in control, the words of my well-practised script tripping easily off my tongue.

'Well,' Crystal began, 'this girl Britney, she thinks I'm a pure muppet, right, because I saw her with this boy who was messaging me ...'

'Sorry, Crystal –' it was probably best to clarify my intentions before the Britney saga reached its epic conclusion – 'I meant, what's brought you to the hospital?'

'Aaah, sorry, nurse.' I ground my teeth. With all the enormous respect due to nurses, who can be extremely skilled and specialised, being called a nurse is something that grates on midwives like nails on a chalkboard. Our role is as different and distinctive as our title, of which each and every one of us is immensely proud. However, I kept my opinions to myself as Crystal continued.

'I thought I was leaking water in double maths first thing this morning, except technically it wasn't double maths, 'cause I was dogging it, and I was actually with my pal Tammy getting a McDonald's, and we were just sitting down with our McMuffins when I was like, holy shit, Tammy, my pants are soaking, I think I've just pished myself. And she was like, that's fucking rank, and I was like, I know but I need to go to the hospital, so we went back to my house to get my bag and feed my rabbits and then Tammy's brother Dean dropped me off in his van, which is *seriously* rank, and Tammy had to get back for fourth-period geography, so yeah.'

'Right.' Head slightly swimming from Crystal's exhaustive history, I remembered the blood-pressure cuff in my hand and wrapped it round Crystal's skinny arm, pulling it as tight as it would go. I mentally composed my documentation for this case: *Patient began draining liquor in McDonald's.* Unlikely though it may have sounded, I had also recently looked after *'patient who lost consciousness in the middle aisle of Lidl'* and *'patient who ruptured her membranes while pushing trolley in Asda'.* The worlds of retail and obstetrics collide much more frequently than the general public might imagine.

'So is the baby coming today, nurse?' Crystal asked as I went through the usual sequence of checking her blood pressure, pulse, temperature and respirations.

'Hopefully not,' I replied. I put my handheld Sonicaid to her tummy and heard the reassuring thump, thump, thump of the baby's heartbeat. 'You're not contracting, but we need you to show us your sanitary pads every time you change them, so that we can see if there's actually amniotic fluid coming away. Sometimes you can be leaking normal discharge or urine, and it feels pretty much the same.' Crystal looked at me in shock, as if I had just asked her to turn her vagina inside out. 'You want to see my fanny pads?' she gasped, then rolled her eyes. 'Some job you've got, nurse.'

The general public may think that midwifery is all baby-catching and biscuits, but behind the scenes a million midwives are paired off in corners and cupboards, showing each other soiled sanitary pads and comparing their colour, consistency and smell in order to make a correct diagnosis and obstetric plan.

'We just need to have a look,' I explained. 'Only to be sure there's nothing unusual going on. You let me know if there's any water or blood, or if you have any pains. There's a buzzer next to your bed and one in the loo if you need it. You can also come and find me … I'll never be far away.' I hesitated as an expression of undisguised adolescent disgust settled on Crystal's face. It occurred to me that this conversation might be easier if Crystal's mother, or an auntie or a friend, was here at her side – someone who'd been down this road before and could reassure her that my unusual demands were not so unusual after all. Should I ask? I wondered. I should.

'Crystal,' I began, 'is your mum or … is there someone who can come down here to sit with you? Just, you know, for company?'

She squirmed on the bed and flicked her phone's screen on and off restlessly – the phone had buzzed about six times while she'd been giving me her story. With my own teenage daughter at home, I had long been oblivious to the constant buzz and ping of a million social media alerts.

'I texted my mum on the way here but she doesn't finish work till ten and, even then, she would have to take two buses to get here, so …' Crystal's voice trailed off, and the briefest shadow furrowed her brow. 'What am I even meant to do all day anyway, nurse?' She tilted her chin up, bold and brash again in an instant. 'I mean, is there even a WiFi password?'

I hated to break it to Crystal, but in spite of the posters all over the wards with the details of the public WiFi network, the hospital set-up was notoriously glitchy and unreliable. Money was about to be poured into a shiny new IT system that would allegedly enable the hospital to go 'paper-lite', if not entirely paper-free, but in the meantime, WiFi, beds, staffing and pretty much every resource going were in need of a major cash infusion. 'There's no money in the pot,' we had been informed with breezy humour at a recent staff meeting; the news hardly came as a surprise.

I left Crystal with a wedge of hospital-issue, boat-like sanitary pads and firm instructions to press the call button if there was anything unusual coming away down below. With a cheery 'Aye, nurse,' she tucked the pads under one arm, repositioned her phone on her knees and launched into another FaceTime. As I moved on to the next room, I could still hear Crystal nattering away behind her curtain: 'Check out the size of these fanny pads, Dean, it's going to be like wearing fucking Pampers.' Her laughter echoed at my back, and I couldn't help but smile. *Got to hand it to her,* I mused. *The girl's got a way with words.*

For the next few hours, the afternoon passed like any other in the antenatal ward. At 2 p.m., a clutch of women arrived for the day's induction list and were promptly dispersed to various rooms around the ward, trailing wheeled suitcases and anxious partners behind them. Every day, women arrive to have their labours kick-started for any number of reasons, from overdue babies, to babies whose movements have slowed, to babies who have already grown so fearsomely chubby that to postpone vaginal birth much longer would mean certain death for the mother's pelvic floor, and a lifetime aversion to trampolines. And so, as cool afternoon light cast slanting shadows across the ward, June and I dotted from bed to bed, tagging each patient with a white name band and wrapping blue elastic CTG belts around each ballooning belly. Woman by woman, we recited the familiar Song of Induction: *You are here because we need to get you into labour, and we have ways of making you do this, and this is how it goes – pessary, pessary, pessary, broken waters, drip.*

June and I glided across the ward like smiling angels of pain, reciting this incantation and popping in Prostin pessaries with a light touch made even lighter by the sachets of lubricant we carried in our tunic pockets, warming them with our body heat (a small but achievable kindness, as anyone who's felt the shocking splodge of a cold-jellied speculum will attest). As we weaved from woman to woman, Crystal made an occasional appearance in our afternoon ballet, now dancing down the corridor to the toilet with pad in one hand and phone in the other, now returning from a trip to the vending machines with an armful of Quavers and Diet Coke. At five o'clock, as I stood at the midwives' station in the middle of the ward, writing up my notes, I felt a tap on my shoulder. It was Crystal. She had accessorised her Mickey Mouse pyjamas with a pair of large neon-orange headphones and was bopping her head in time to their tinny beat.

'All right, Crystal?' I enquired.

'Dry as a bone, sister,' she said a little too loudly and grinned, pointing to her crotch.

'Good,' I replied. 'Let's keep it that way.'

As Crystal bounced back down the corridor towards her room and I raised my pen to continue scribbling my notes (*Patient reports nil further fluid per vaginam, mobilising well around the ward*), I saw a familiar figure bustling towards me: five foot one, swamped in scrubs three sizes too big and a navy blue headscarf, gleaming white trainers squeaking along the polished floor at a businesslike clip.

'*Salaam alaikum*, girls,' said the doctor, sighing as she approached the midwives' station. Soraya, one of the senior obstetric registrars, had come to our hospital from Abu Dhabi the previous year and had already earned widespread respect among the staff for her no-nonsense attitude and razor-sharp clinical judgement. The traditional Arabic greeting was as far as Soraya's pleasantries went – after that, it was just the facts, ma'am.

'What have you got for me?' she asked as she surveyed the piles of notes strewn across the desk. 'And what is all this?' she said, rifling through the chaotic pages in front of her. 'Has there been an explosion?'

June popped her head out of an adjacent room. 'Nothing from me, doctor. All the afternoon Prostins are done, just one patient niggling and another two on the birth balls. And the placenta praevia in room nine's nipped out for a smoke.'

Soraya rolled her eyes and turned to me. 'And you?' The pager clipped to her waistband let out a series of shrill beeps. 'Make it quick. I need to scrub for a ruptured ectopic.'

I thought of mentioning Crystal but, as the girl herself had said, she was dry as a bone – no more waters leaking, no contractions, tiny fetus still swimming in its cosy bubble. Maybe the whole thing had been a false alarm. 'Nothing really, Soraya ...'

'That's what I like to hear,' she called over her shoulder as she turned on a squeaky heel and began to speed back towards the lifts, raising a hand in a weary half-wave as she went. 'Keep it good for me, girls. Keep it good.'

It was half past six, just over an hour until the end of my shift, and I clicked smoothly into autopilot as the day began to draw to a close. It was time to tidy those loose notes and do one last tour of the ward to check on my patients, refreshing water jugs, dispensing clean pads and murmuring final words of encouragement as I went. The ward was beginning to thrum with the low, crampy moans of early labour; that afternoon's inductions were crossing en masse into the seductive shadowlands of pain, and as I passed by each doorway, I could see women rocking in slow circles on big pink birth balls, partners rubbing smaller circles on their backs, faces fixed in watchful anticipation. With any luck, the real dramas would start on the night shift – contractions rippling through the ward room by room, women hurtling towards the desk with hastily tied, hospital-issue gowns flapping behind them, desperate to know why there were six women ahead of them in the queue for labour ward, unaware that there were no empty rooms and no free midwives and hours still to go.

'NURSE!' I froze as I cleared a dinner tray from the room next to Crystal's. There was no mistaking the voice. I rushed into room six to find Crystal standing in the middle of the floor, pyjama bottoms and knickers pulled down to her knees, with a steady trickle of olive-green liquid running down her thighs.

It was unmistakeable: amniotic fluid mixed with meconium, the murky, sticky poo that builds up inside the fetus's gut during pregnancy, sometimes released when the baby is overdue, but also sometimes expelled when the baby is in a state of metabolic distress. In other words: oh, shit.

'What's happening, nurse?' There was a new, brittle edge to her voice and the colour had drained from her face. Terror had replaced bravado. The curtains along the back wall ruffled and sighed with a breeze and as the drab, pale-pistachio fabric settled back into place, I became suddenly aware of the winter chill in the room. Every window had been opened. The whole scene was deeply wrong – a child with the ripe, round belly of a woman, a cold space on a warm ward, muddy drops of fluid raining onto a smooth, polished floor – and my vision swam with the incongruity of it all for one long, seasick moment before my midwife brain took over.

I moved swiftly across the floor and put an arm around Crystal's shoulders, shuffling her back towards the bed. 'Let's get you lying down on your side,' I said, taking care over every word, hoping my voice wouldn't betray the panic that had fluttered in my chest. 'You can tell me what happened, and then we'll get some help.'

'I was just opening the windows,' she said as I eased her down onto the mattress. I drew the blue thermal blanket up under Crystal's chin; the cheap waffle-weave flickered with static, as it always did, and we both flinched. 'I was going to have a cheeky fag – you know, just the one – and I went to open the last window, and …'

'And it started coming out?'

Crystal nodded in reply.

'And does anything feel different now? Are you sore?'

'Aye, nurse,' she said. 'I feel like I need to do a giant jobbie, but it's not coming.'

Double shit. Rectal pressure is often a sign that there's a baby sitting right down on your bowel, which is next door to your vagina, which for a twenty-three-week baby is a one-way route to trouble. I looked down at the fob watch pinned to my chest; ten minutes to seven. *18.50,* I noted to myself. *Copious Grade Two meconium draining per vaginam.* And then, out loud, to Crystal, 'Listen to me. You need to stay right here. Stay warm. I'm going to go and get the other midwife, and …'

At this, her eyes grew wide. 'But my baby! What are they going to do to my baby?'

The honest answer was, I didn't know. Crystal looked smaller than ever; her fear had made her recede into the pillows, diminishing her with every passing second. As words whirled and faltered in my head, I instinctively reached out to sweep the thick cloud of hair away from her face. These gestures – the drawing of the blanket, the reaching out – were automatic, had been practised many times with my own children in my own home. The curl of a small body under a quilt, the quiver of a frightened lip – these images triggered a response in me that required no thought or explanation. Comfort: this was what the mother in me had learned to provide long before midwifery had even entered my life, and this was the only thing I could reliably offer to Crystal at the moment when her world began to shatter.

'I'm going to let the labour ward know that they'll be seeing us soon,' I said, my face close to Crystal's, speaking as slowly and clearly as my nerves would allow. 'If anything exciting happens, press your buzzer.'

Before I could be drawn into any further discussion or delay, I turned on my heel and raced back towards the desk, where June was finishing her day's documentation.

'The PPROM's leaking meconium, and she's got rectal pressure.'

June's head whipped up; her eyes narrowed to jet-black beads. 'What time do you call this for an emergency? There's an ice-cold G&T waiting for me at home and there's no way I'm staying late for the third bloody time this week.'

I sighed, and looked again at my fob watch. It was now eight minutes to seven, but every minute was critical, even during that foggy window at the end of a shift when the staff are still physically present but have mentally checked out, already planning their dinner (and 'purely medicinal' drinks) while they perform the last ministrations of the day.

'I know, June,' I said. 'I'm sorry.'

In unison, we each picked up a telephone.

'I'll call labour suite, you call the paeds.'

I could hear June telling the emergency paediatric staff the bare bones of Crystal's story. 'Of course we've let labour ward know,' June said, looking pointedly at me. The labour ward line was still ringing out. 'We're getting her up as soon as we can.'

Nobody was answering my call. Anything could be happening; there could be six emergencies going on at once, the staff could all be in theatre, the day-shift sister could be squeezing in a late break, kicking off her shoes and curling up with a steaming mug of tea while the night-shift sister surveyed the whiteboard in the bunker. My thoughts turned to the Resuscitaire at the back of the ward – I imagined Crystal's scrawny baby gasping and flailing under the heat lamp as I scrambled in vain for a mouthpiece tiny enough to administer vital oxygen, and then I imagined myself losing my job for even attempting to resuscitate a twenty-three-weeker, and then I imagined how I would never forgive myself if I hadn't even tried. In my relatively short career, I already knew midwives who had been investigated, suspended or sanctioned for less; the spectre of disciplinary action hovers at the edges of every midwife's thoughts, taunting her most loudly in her weakest, darkest moments. The images in my mind grew more nightmarish with every unanswered ring of the phone. I could hear Crystal sobbing from her room. *Pick up, pick up, pick up.*

'Labour ward sister,' came a tired voice down the line.

I nearly collapsed with relief. 'I'm on my way with a twenty-three and three PPROM, draining meconium, feeling rectal pressure. Paeds are aware.' I slammed the phone down, not waiting for an answer.

June was already at Crystal's bedside, where a pool of cloudy, algal fluid had begun to seep through Crystal's pyjama bottoms and was spreading ominously over the sheets. She kicked up the footbrake at the bottom of the frame and we heaved the bed with Crystal on it out of the room, through the ward's doors and out towards the lifts. June punched the lift button so hard I thought she would break it, while Crystal continued to wail.

'Will they save my baby, nurse? Will they keep my baby alive? What will I aaaaaagggh ...' and she curled into a ball with a long, low grunt. June and I eyeballed each other across the bed as the lift finally creaked open. The journey up seemed to take hours, Crystal's cries echoing around the metal box as it lurched and ground to a halt. The second the doors opened onto the top-floor foyer, we were already hurling the bed out, arms and shoulders aching, weaving through a cluster of day-shift staff who were making an early exit down the adjacent stairwell.

'Excuse us, coming through,' we called as we went. When you're transferring a patient in an emergency, people always seem to move out of your way in painful slow-motion, with an almost comical lack of urgency, scarcely raising an eyebrow as you bounce the bed off corners and walls at breakneck speed.

Finally, the labour ward. June and I tapped our badges frantically off the keypad at its entrance and the double doors swung to the sides. The night-shift sister was waiting for us, along with two paediatricians and Soraya, whose dark eyes were blazing from beneath her hijab. Every face glared at me with an unmistakeable, unspoken message: *It's Your Fault.* I knew it wasn't – I had as much control over Crystal's cervix as I do over global stock markets or El Niño – but in that moment, it felt as though I was the worst midwife ever, the bearer of bad news, of crisis and complication, of patients with misbehaving uteruses, inconveniently timed contractions, of cervixes that decide to spring open when they should be rosebud-tight. The staff glared at me with silent rage, as if I had presented them with a steaming turd, not a terrified child who was about to become a mother to a small, skinny thing that might or might not live beyond its first few desperate gasps. At the increasingly frequent times when the sheer volume of patients outstrips the number of available beds and midwives, the criteria for admission to the labour ward – that mecca of maternity – become impossibly (and often cruelly) narrow. Women who are contracting frequently but coping well may be dismissed by the notorious sister who expects all labourers to be – to use her charming expression – 'rolling around like a beast'. In busy spells, uncomfortable pretermers can be viewed with suspicion until their tightenings are convincingly agonising, and woe betide the midwife who arrives at the labour ward doors at short notice, murmuring sweet nothings to her panicking patient even though she knows full well that there's no room at the inn. I had encountered this hostile reception many times, but it never got any easier to accept or to hide from the women who thought they'd finally found – and earned – a place of comfort and safety.

Crystal might have been scared, but she wasn't blind, and she quickly clocked the expressions of those who had met her at the door. She rose up on the bed, flung her arms around my waist and cried, 'What will they do? Will they save my baby? Is it too soon?'

Crystal's hair had billowed back onto her face; again, I smoothed it away, and this time she tilted her cheek almost imperceptibly towards my palm, leaning into whatever last fragments of love I could offer. I had no answers to her questions and, even if I had, there was no time to give them. Midwives soon learn that it's never a good idea to tell patients that everything will be OK, because the truth is that it might not be. Nature is cruel. The homespun wisdom that 'babies come when they're ready' is a lie: babies come when they're ready, and also when they're not, and sometimes it's OK, but sometimes it really, really isn't. Hard experience teaches the midwife that only a fool would promise a happy ending every time.

Soraya grabbed the foot of the bed, the labour ward sister grabbed the top, and I felt Crystal's arms slip away from my waist as they launched her towards the first available room. The double doors swung shut and I stood in the foyer, alone. I could hear the laughter of midwives down the stairs as they continued their evening exodus. 'I told him to stop wasting his time,' said a voice, and there was a chorus of gravelly cackles followed by the slam of a fire door, and then silence.

It was seven twenty-eight. June had trotted back towards the lift as soon as we had dispatched Crystal, and I knew she would be down in the ward already, expecting me to return and hand over the rest of my patients to the night staff, reporting on this one's incoordinate contractions and that one's penicillin allergy. I couldn't face it. I felt as if one of my own children had been rushed to theatre, grabbing onto my heartstrings as she went; I could almost feel them pinging and snapping in my chest. I didn't know if Crystal's baby would survive, or even if the paediatric team would attempt what was casually referred to as 'heroics': intubation, cannulation, drugs and every possible intervention that might give a baby a chance of surviving for an hour, a day or even longer. So much depended on whether Crystal's estimated due date was even correct to begin with – was she really just twenty-three weeks and three days, or five days or six? And on whether her baby came out in vigorous condition, and on whether the attending staff decided to stride boldly into the no-man's land of the twenty-three-weeker or if they chose to hang back among the clear, comforting black-and-white guide-lines of the law.

My head began to throb as I travelled down to the ground floor, trying (and failing) to avoid my haggard reflection in the lift's mirrored interior. I let myself into the changing room, put my coat on over my uniform and slipped out of a side door into the car park. As I fumbled for my car keys, I felt a piece of thick paper in my pocket. I pulled it out. Two ducks hugging, with hearts above their heads. Mrs Bhatti's card. I moved into a pool of light cast by one of the street lamps and peered down. *Quack you very much*, it read. Then, in my own handwriting, *Thank you so much for all of your hard work.*

The words were mine, the thought was Mrs Bhatti's. Hot tears slid down my cheeks. I wasn't due back at the hospital for another four days; four days of doing normal things, being Mum, making packed lunches and cooking dinners, and marking my day by dog walks and loads of laundry, shuttling from washer to drier instead of from bed to bed. Four days of wondering about Crystal and her baby – that small, scrawny sketch of a human. I slipped the card back into my pocket and began to search through the darkness for my car.

Notes on Paper Pants and Broken Dreams

The postnatal ward is a place where dreams are made and broken. You arrive on the ward with your precious cargo swaddled in layers of blankets like a mewling, cottony burrito. You've waited nine months to meet little Oliver or Maya or Mohammed or Kate, and in spite of the fact that your baby bears all of the less attractive hallmarks of labour (a remarkably cone-shaped head daubed with poo, blood or vernix – or a fragrant mixture of all three), you are 100 per cent convinced that this child is the Most Beautiful Cherub Ever to Grace the Planet. Your labour ward midwife shows you to your bed space – perhaps pushing you on a wheelchair with two suitcases and seven poly bags draped over its handles or birling you into position on an almost unmanoeuvrable bed whose brakes were last serviced in 1972, whanging you off every corner and doorway en route. ('Learner driver!' she laughs by way of an apology as you try to make yourself as compact and un-whangable as possible.) She gives you one last hug, tells you how amazing you are and chirps, 'See you in two years!' – which makes your perineum sting just thinking about it – before leaving you in the care of your postnatal midwife. Prior to your appearance on the ward, this woman with the strained smile and drooping ponytail has already done four discharges and two admissions, missed a break and now been asked to look after the mother of preterm twins in room eight whose babies are both on three-hourly observations and IV antibiotics. The exhaustion is written on her face as she checks your vital signs and hands you a sheaf of booklets about an overwhelming array of topics ranging from the prevention of cot death to car seats to breastfeeding and beyond, as well as a chart you are instructed to complete (black pen only, please) every time your little cherub feeds, vomits or graces its nappy with a slug of sticky poo. Unfortunately, you have arrived on the ward on a particularly busy afternoon. And although your midwife would genuinely love to help you feed your baby (now hungry, and thus transformed from a cooing angel to a screaming child of Satan), she is quickly interrupted by: 1) Patient A, who has been 'nipping out for fresh air' all day but suddenly seems to have lost the use of her limbs and wants the midwife to pick her used sanitary pads up off the floor; 2) Patient B, whose thumb appears to have become welded to her call button; and 3) Patient C's husband, who finds it completely unacceptable that the staff are too busy to reheat his wife's Happy Meal, and reminds the midwife in no uncertain terms that he is a Very Important Person with Impressive Medical Credentials. (NB: a quick flick through Patient C's case notes reveals that Mr C is, in actual fact, the assistant manager of a dental surgery.)

Your midwife smiles weakly at you before excusing herself to see to these urgent demands, promising over her shoulder that she'll be back before you know it. You smile lopsidedly in return as her stooped figure disappears behind the blue paper curtain and you pray that you have been charming enough during that brief interaction for your midwife to understand that you're actually a very nice person, and you know how busy she is, and you really, really hope that when you do finally muster the nerve to press your own call button, she will respond with speed and goodwill and maybe, just maybe, an extra packet of those cheap shortbread biscuits that you only ever seem to get in hospitals. On the other side of the ward, your midwife notices that one of her patients is bleeding a little too much and as she reaches for the emergency buzzer she has a fleeting thought of you, and a pang of guilt, knowing that she probably won't be able to get to your bedside again until this haemorrhage and the teatime drugs round and visiting time are over.

Outside your room, a trolley rumbles by on squeaking wheels, followed by a pungent waft of – could it be fish pie? Dinner has arrived somewhere on the ward, but finding it would be hard with legs still dense from the epidural you begged for early that morning. (Did you offer the handsome young anaesthetist some pretty creative favours in return for a denser block? It's a distinct possibility and you blush at the memory.) Your stomach grumbles and you gingerly shift the weight of your baby from one arm to the other, leaving you with a free hand to rummage under the sheets for your buzzer, which you've now decided to press, just this once, very lightly, so as not to be a nuisance. As your hand grasps wildly under the bedsheets, it brushes against the vast paper pants that the labour ward midwife hoisted valiantly up your legs a few short hours ago and you remember the advice given to you in soothing tones by your mother last week at your baby shower, which now seems like it happened to another woman, in another life.

'Don't worry if things don't go the way you planned, dear,' she had said. 'At the end of the day, the only thing that matters is a healthy baby.'

This, of course, is a truism. The whole point of reproduction, biologically speaking, is to create healthy offspring. However, a baby's journey to wellbeing doesn't stop at delivery. In order to forge a cast-iron bond between mother and child, nature drugs women who have just given birth with a hormone that makes them feel warm and fuzzy, blissed out, loved up – the same hormone that started labour in the first place, that's felt in the very first flashes of love and, in one super-condensed, mind-bending burst, in the throes of orgasm. Love, lust and contractions: all brought to you by none other than our sponsor, oxytocin.

By rights, then, the postnatal ward should be a shrine to oxytocin, a laid-back love shack where mother and baby can gaze at each other gooey-eyed for hours, with noise and distractions kept to a bare minimum. Unfortunately, as new mothers come to realise on so many levels, reality doesn't always match up to the ideal. Postnatal care is often referred to as the 'Cinderella' sector of maternity services because, like the princess whose ball gown turns to rags at the stroke of midnight, much of the idealism and joy of a woman's journey frequently seems to evaporate once the actual birth is over and done with. The mythical 'glow' of pregnancy is replaced by the nitty-gritty of throbbing ladyparts, leaking breasts and dirty nappies. Put Cinderella in an understaffed, underfunded maternity hospital, where she is one of many women whose silks have turned to sackcloth, and you begin to get the picture. The fairy dust of oxytocin is still there, scattered in tiny, sparkling clumps over bedpans and breast pumps, but it's no match for the hulking, grinding gears of the maternity machine.

There are, of course, exceptions to that depressing rule. Sometimes Cinderella *does* go to the ball and sometimes it is still possible for the postnatal ward to provide the kind of cocoon that women deserve. Every once in a great while, when the stars are aligned, and the birth rate slows to a manageable stride and the wards themselves seem to breathe an audible sigh of relief, it looks a little bit like this:

You arrive just after midnight, your wheelchair gliding down darkened corridors, past dimly lit bays of sleeping women and their infants, until you reach – you can hardly believe your eyes – a private room. The bedside lamp is turned to the wall, casting a soft, cosy glow over the bed, with its crisp white sheets turned back invitingly, and the waiting cot sits nearby, its drawers fully stocked with fluffy towels and miniature clouds of cotton wool. On the far wall, a window looks out onto the darkness beyond the hospital, city lights twinkling faintly in the distance, and you are overwhelmed by a rush of gratitude for this warm, safe place, this little pod which seems to have been magicked up especially for this moment, for you and the adorable, sweetly scented baby in your arms. 'Welcome to the ward,' says a gentle voice behind you, and as you rise slowly out of the wheelchair, child still clutched to your chest, you turn to see the smiling, blue-tunicked postnatal midwife who will be your guardian angel for the night. She moves to help you lay your baby gently in the cot, cradling his head with the lightest touch, and as she does so, you catch her warm scent of perfume and sweet tea. You don't know it, but your midwife has had one of those rare nights when she's had only a handful of patients and she's been able to stop a while at each bedside, chatting and soothing with an unpushed ease that makes her heart sing. She's even had a proper break, instead of the usual rushed tea-and-biscuit over a pile of case notes: tonight, she's had a chance to sit in the office with the other night staff, admiring the photos of this one's grandchildren, stifling laughter at that one's filthy jokes, and taking time to pick all of the coffee creams from the boxes of chocolates left by the day shift's discharged patients. By the time you've arrived on the ward, she's been reminded of a feeling she hasn't had in a long while: the feeling that she's actually good at her job when she gets the time and the space to do it properly, and that it's about so, so much more than healthy babies alone.

Olivia:
Mother Knows Best

It was my first of three day shifts on the postnatal ward, and by the time it came to the afternoon drugs round, the Fat Bastards Club had already taken its toll. As I heaved the trolley full of medicines from room to room, my legs seemed to trail heavily behind me, trainers dragging along the linoleum floor in protest.

Terri, one of the ward's auxiliaries, had started the club at the end of the summer. Shocked by the sudden expanse of her waistline after consuming slightly more than her fair share of barbequed meats and beer-garden tipples, Terri had sat at the desk at 2 a.m. one night and opened a fresh spiral-bound notepad with a flourish. *Fat Bastards Club*, she had written at the top of the first page and, underneath it, her own credentials in proud print: *Terri, 13 stone 6 pounds, September 4*. Within the week, she had persuaded every other staff member in the ward to add their names and weights to the list and devised an on-the-job fitness routine which we were all instructed, in no uncertain terms, to follow. Whenever we had a break or a rare quiet spell on the ward, we were to climb up and down the hospital's five flights of stairs at least three times. Between making beds and doing the tea round, Terri took great delight in checking on her colleagues' progress. You could be in the drug prep room, tapping the bubbles out of a syringe of antibiotics, and Terri's grinning face would appear around the door frame.

'You been doing your stairs?' she would ask, and if the answer was anything but a resounding yes, she would put a black mark next to your name in the Fat Bastards Club notebook and personally corral you into a stair-climbing session. At first, there were a few resistant folk – those who had tried to 'be good' over the summer or who were already diehard members of Slimming World, Weight Watchers or one of the many diet clubs that midwives seem to flock to with varying degrees of success – but we all followed Terri's orders in the end. Not only was she a five-foot-one, thirteen-stone whirlwind of persuasion, but as midwives, we seemed to take naturally to the futile routine of climbing the stairs to the storerooms on the top floor, only to climb back down and start again. We were already accustomed to working ourselves into a state of semi-comatose exhaustion every day, only to return in the morning and repeat the process with a completely fresh batch of patients. For every catheter emptied, there was another bag waiting to be filled up with pungent, postnatal urine; for every woman discharged, there were five more waiting to be admitted. Thus, as early autumn cast a subtle chill over the hospital, it became the norm to find midwives marching in pairs up and down the stairs at two o'clock in the morning, or half past four in the afternoon, or whenever the shift's workload had eased up enough for us to do our duty as repentant Fat Bastards.

Terri came to find me that day as I was returning the drugs trolley to its home, safely tethered to a locked shackle on the wall of the prep room. My drawstring trousers had only needed a little loosening after the indulgence of the summer holidays, but I had been doing the stairs with unquestioning obedience on every shift.

'Done them already today,' I said to Terri when she appeared in the doorway, before she even had the chance to question me. 'My legs are agony.'

'Good girl,' Terri replied, approvingly. 'But I've just come to tell you that the hospital coordinator's been on the phone. She wants to put someone into room eight – prim, emergency section, coming up on a bed. I'll clear a space.' She disappeared for a moment before popping her face back round the doorway. 'Weigh-in tomorrow, by the way. The girls in Outpatients are going to let us borrow their scales.' She grinned and darted off again, battered Reeboks squeaking towards room eight as she went.

I began to assemble the bits and pieces I would need for my admission: a jug of fresh water, a clean cot, a small metal stand on which to hang the catheter bag that any post-Caesarean patient was bound to have. I paused next to the stacks of leaflets by the filing cabinet in the staff base: there was one set for breastfeeders and another for bottle-feeders, but I didn't know which ones this new mother would need. It was a cardinal sin to give a bottle-feeder the breast-feeding pamphlets (this gaffe would confirm any midwife's status as a fully fledged member of the mythical, much-maligned 'Breastfeeding Gestapo', thus stirring the patient into a frenzy of guilt or anger) and it was virtually a sackable offence to give the bottle-feeding booklets to a breastfeeder, so keen was our ward on the promotion of the Boob for any mother minded to try it.

When she was wheeled onto the ward twenty minutes later, Olivia was little more than a frazzled husk tucked among a tangle of sheets and drips; she had laboured for nearly thirty-six hours and reached full dilatation, only for her baby (who was now crying lustily in her arms) to become distressed and in need of immediate delivery. Her face was milky pale and her strawberry-blonde hair lay in limp strands across her pillow. She barely had the energy to lift her head and peer at the noisy bundle in her arms. A bag of IV fluids trickled into a cannula on Olivia's left hand, a coil of catheter tubing snaked round her legs in a golden snarl at the bottom of the bed, and a quick peek under the sheets revealed a wodge of hastily folded bed mats jammed between her legs to soak up her postnatal bleeding. In short, Olivia was typical of so many of the patients who arrived on the ward, and she reminded me very much of my younger self after the birth of my first daughter. I had been so zonked by blood loss and fatigue that when my cannula finally fell out on day four, I begged the midwives to put it back in so that I could keep mainlining the morphine that had been keeping me in a comfortably numb fog since delivery. To this day, I have never met another woman who actually wanted her IV replaced; most patients are delighted to be rid of that niggly little tube in their vein.

'Welcome to the ward,' I said, bustling around Olivia, doing my usual sequence of baseline observations. Her husband Paul attempted to shuffle out of my way as I moved alongside the bed, but between the bedside cabinet, the chair, Olivia's suitcases, the cot and the bed itself, there was barely enough space for all of us within the curtained bay. Paul and I blushed and murmured awkward apologies as we danced around each other, and through it all, the baby screamed an increasingly urgent crescendo.

'Should I feed her, do you think?' Olivia asked weakly. 'She had something downstairs, but it wasn't much.'

The baby's face was beetroot with rage and hunger; it was time for the million-dollar question. 'Are you breast- or bottle-feeding?' I asked breezily, hoping my tone was neutral enough not to betray any bias. It's one of the most loaded questions a midwife can ask her patient, right up there with 'What are your thoughts about pain relief?' and 'Do you smoke?' As someone who formula-fed one baby after a painful, guilt-ridden struggle with breastfeeding, then breastfed another child for over two years with almost unbelievable ease, I have no personal agenda other than a desire to facilitate whatever choice a woman wants to make. Yes, current evidence confirms that the breast is undeniably best for the health of both mother and baby, but a woman's preference – and whether it really is 'best' for her and her child – is influenced by a myriad of factors, not all of them tangible or easily explained, and many of which will remain unknown to her midwife. I've never been one to enter into this debate with a patient who, more often than not, has made up her mind many months before she arrives in my care. Woman chooses, baby's belly is full. No questions asked, no judgement made. Job done.

Olivia peered up at Paul, who was now wedged beside the head of the bed. It was a look I recognised well: both a question and a request for forgiveness.

'Well, we were going to breastfeed –' my teeth clenched at the 'we'; much as parenting can be a joint enterprise, lactation is pretty exclusively a female occupation – 'but I'm just so tired, I think I'll give her a bottle,' Olivia said, sighing. She lifted up her free, non-cannulated hand to stroke her baby's cheek and then looked up at me, adding apologetically, 'If it's OK with you.'

I smiled down at her from my position at the foot of the bed. 'Whatever you want to do is fine by me,' I said. Olivia looked surprised, and then relieved. Even her shoulders seemed to drop incrementally; her whole body had been bracing itself for my disapproval. It saddened me to think that Olivia had prepared herself for a battle, even after everything else her battered body had been through, but again, this was a response I knew well.

'Thanks,' Paul added. He pushed a stray hair back from Olivia's chalk-white face. 'It's just that I work on the rigs and I've already been off for two weeks, so I have to head up to Aberdeen tomorrow morning, and then back out. Olivia's mum will be here to help, but we need to do whatever's easiest.' He squeezed Olivia's arm. 'I had no idea that birth could be like that – all those hours of labour, and then major surgery. I think I'm still in shock.'

'You and me both, pal,' Olivia replied.

I nodded in sympathy. 'What kind of milk would you like?' I asked, and then listed the three brands of formula we had on the ward. 'I can't really say which one is best, it's up to you.'

'Surprise me,' Olivia said, as she busied herself with adjusting the pink woolly hat on her baby's head, and just like that, her choice was made. I hurried off to the room where the formula was kept, rather disingenuously, in a cupboard labelled *Breastfeeding Supplies*, and returned with the first bottle of milk I had seen on the shelf. By this time, Paul was sitting in the chair at Olivia's bedside with the baby in his arms; he took the bottle from me and the baby's cries settled almost instantly into grateful snuffles as he nudged the teat between her lips. Outside the curtain, the usual crowd of evening visitors had begun to file noisily into the ward, but Olivia was oblivious: exhaustion swept over her in a wave. As her baby slurped and gurgled happily at her side, Olivia's eyes drooped shut, her jaw slackened and her body sank into a deep, dreamless sleep.

My own sleep that night was a restless one. All of the characters in the ward's daily dramas came to life as my mind digested the shift – their roles swapped to absurd effect and their dialogue twisted into an incomprehensible babble. In my dreams, midwives ran down endless corridors towards some far-off emergency, and no matter how many times I consulted the folded to-do list in my tunic pocket, my dream-self spent the night fretting over missed medications, crying babies and patients whose call buttons set off loud, clanging alarm bells instead of the usual droning buzz.

By the time I arrived on the ward the next day, I was little more than a sleepwalker in uniform. As I attempted to fix my bed-blasted hair in the mirror of the staff toilets, I reflected that I must have woken up, dressed, had breakfast and driven myself to the hospital, but I could barely remember any of it. Nerys, another midwife on the day shift, recognised my Groundhog Day glaze when she came into the room: 'Same old shit, different shovel,' she said, squeezing my arm. Our reflections grinned ruefully back at us in the mirror.

The day's first coffee began to drip its jittery energy into my veins as I walked the ward, checking on the patients I knew and introducing myself to those who had been admitted overnight. As I came to Olivia's room, I could hear her speaking in low, urgent conversation with another woman whose voice I didn't recognise.

'Just let me try it like this, Mum,' Olivia was saying.

'I don't think you're doing it right, dear. If you just move your hands a hair's breadth this way …'

There was the sound of a minor scuffle, and a baby's frustrated yowl.

'Mum, just let me …'

'If you'd only let me help, Olivia. You've always been a bit ham-fisted.'

The voices stopped as soon as I drew back the curtain to find Olivia and her mother frozen in a furious, mute tableau, like squabbling toddlers caught fighting over a coveted toy; only in this case, the object of their tug-of-war was a baby who was very much alive, furiously darting its tongue around in hungry protest. To my surprise, the baby was scrabbling at Olivia's bare breasts; her pink flannelette pyjama top lay wide open and tiny globules of milk hung from each of her nipples. This was a stark contrast to her mother, whose sudden, fixed grin at my arrival was as steely as the grey, kirby-gripped bun on the top of her head, and whose own pink cashmere cardigan was tightly buttoned right up to the string of pearls around her neck.

'Ah, *there* she is,' said Olivia's mother, cooing in mock delight, clasping her hands together. 'The wonderful nurse that my daughter's been telling me all about.'

'Midwife, actually,' I said, matching her tone. I had the measure of this woman. I flashed her a smile, quick but every bit as steely as her own, and turned to her daughter. 'How are you this morning, Olivia?' I asked, pointedly.

Olivia returned a wan smile and hoisted the baby, who had been dressed in a blush-pink Babygro and matching hat, closer to her chest. 'I'm fine, thanks,' she said. 'My mum's spending the day with me because Paul's headed back to work.'

'Only the day, mind you,' her mother chimed. 'I can't leave Olivia's father for too long, nurse. You know what these men are like when left to their own devices.' She gave a conspiratorial wink. 'He hardly knows the microwave from the Hoover, poor thing. My fault, of course. I do spoil him terribly.'

I gave her another fleeting smile and turned back to Olivia. 'How was your night?'

'Well, I was pretty sore,' she began, 'so I think I was up for most of it ...'

'Yes, well, that's the way with these Caesars,' Olivia's mother added, using the antiquated short-hand for a Caesarean section. 'So much harder than giving birth the *right* way.' I raised an eyebrow and Olivia's cheeks blushed scarlet as she looked down at her baby in silent rage, but her mother ploughed on. 'But Livvy's going to do the right thing now, aren't you, darling? So from here on, we're breastfeeding.'

By this point, both of my eyebrows were raised, and in spite of my desire to remain unruffled under the scrutiny of Olivia's mother, I could barely conceal my surprise. 'We're ... you're breastfeeding?' I asked Olivia, trying to keep my voice steady.

She raised her head and tossed her hair over her shoulder. It had been brushed to a fine gloss, I noticed, and Olivia had even put on some lipstick and blusher, no doubt in an attempt to make herself 'presentable' for her esteemed visitor.

'Yes, I'm breastfeeding,' she confirmed. 'Mum's been ... helping me. But I can't get Rosie to latch,' she said, looking down again at the baby who was now pawing at her breast with increasingly frantic desperation. 'I don't know what I'm doing wrong.'

'That's fine,' I said. Olivia's mother sat back with a satisfied smile. This was a scenario I had encountered many times: a new mother whose baby has already feasted on numerous bottles of formula deciding after a day, or sometimes two or three, that she would like to breastfeed; sometimes it is a genuinely autonomous decision, but more often than not, the choice is influenced by well-meaning but insidiously passive-aggressive comments from visiting friends and family. It is difficult, but not impossible, to breastfeed after the first day or two of lactation have been missed: babies can still squeeze into that precious window of opportunity when their mother's milk-producing hormones are at their highest, but it takes persistence, a commitment to frequent feeding attempts and a willingness to forgo anything resembling normal sleeping patterns until the process is well established. Watching Olivia's baby grasping furious handfuls of her mother's pyjamas, her mouth rooting wildly from left to right but missing the nipple on every pass, I knew we had a long day ahead of us.

'Let's begin at the beginning,' I said to Olivia. 'Is it OK if I squeeze onto the edge of your bed here?' Olivia nodded her assent. Officially, sitting anywhere on a patient's bed is a big Infection Control no-no: who knows what treacherous germs could be lurking on the navy-blue seat of your uniform trousers? However, many a postnatal midwife has sent her back into agonising spasms by leaning precariously over a bedside while attempting to crowbar a patient's breast into her baby's mouth. The goal is admirable, but the process bears more than a passing resemblance to the 'stress positions' notoriously used in modern-day torture; it is so much easier, and more companionable, to sit next to your patient. And so I perched a grateful buttock on the edge of Olivia's bed and gently moved her baby into a safe, secure hold for breastfeeding.

'Tummy to tummy, nose to nipple,' I began, reciting the incantation drilled into every midwife at lactation workshops up and down the land. 'Nice wide mouth, chin tucked under, that's it, pop Rosie's hands out of the way so she doesn't push herself off the breast ...' I kept my smile fixed across my cheeks as Olivia fumbled gamely with her baby under her mother's frosty gaze.

Current trends in midwifery dictate that we're supposed to be 'hands-off' when helping new mums breastfeed. If a midwife puts the baby to the breast herself, instead of allowing the process to happen spontaneously, this 'interference' is said to undermine the mother's confidence. Videos in antenatal classes show newborn babies placed on their mum's abdomen crawling miraculously up to the breast, then locating and latching onto the nipple with the accuracy of a chubby-cheeked guided missile. The reality is often somewhat different, leading women to spend tearful hours wondering why their little Jack or Jamal doesn't do what the baby in the movie did, and leading midwives to spend those same hours sitting on their hands at the bedside, grinning away like demented Cheshire cats while fighting the overwhelming urge to grasp the poor child and latch it to the boob in one fell swoop. So it began with Olivia. I sat with her for half an hour, suggesting a little adjustment here or a tweak there, folding a pillow under her left arm and propping another two behind her shoulders, willing little Rosie to locate the nipple and delight in the rich, creamy colostrum that was trickling temptingly just out of reach, until finally, Rosie's flailing attempts exhausted her so much that she fell asleep in her mother's arms. Olivia sat back dejectedly on her throne of pillows, defeated.

'I don't know if this is going to work,' Olivia said as Rosie's head lolled heavily in her arms. 'I just can't seem to do it.'

Olivia's mother patted her arm. 'There, there, darling. All the best things are worth waiting for,' she replied, her voice dripping with saccharine sympathy. 'I'm sure the nurse will be happy to spend the day helping you. What could possibly be more important than getting this right?'

I bit my tongue so hard that I wondered whether blood would actually start to trickle down my chin and onto my uniform; the stains on my tunic would require some explanation to the ward sister at the midday huddle. Of course I was happy to help Olivia breastfeed if that was really what she wanted, and of course I knew that success was a definite possibility with the right amount of guidance. But this woman's butter-wouldn't-melt attitude was seriously beginning to grate on me, never mind her insistence on calling me 'nurse', which I was starting to think was intentional. Add to this the fact that the ward was heaving – we had been told to open up extra beds to accommodate a spike in deliveries, and my colleagues were already well into their morning workloads – and

I was sure that with all the will in the world, I wouldn't be able to give Olivia the kid-gloved time and effort that her mother was expecting.

'Of course I'd be delighted to do everything I can to help you breastfeed,' I intoned. 'The best thing you can do now is keep little Rosie skin-to-skin, so she can smell all that delicious milk, and then if she does start looking for a feed again, she'll be in the right place at the right time.' This suggestion seemed to satisfy Olivia and her mother, and with a squeaky turn of my heel, I dashed off to begin my long-overdue drugs round.

As the day went on, I did my best to return to Olivia as frequently as I could. Some of these bedside visits were spontaneous, and some were prompted by Olivia's mother pressing the call button every time her granddaughter's mouth drifted within close proximity of a nipple. Each time the buzzer went, I hurried through what I was doing – applying a pressure dressing to a leaky wound or taking out a cannula – and bustled along to Olivia's bed space, only to find Rosie asleep or grizzling through her first poo or pushing her mother's breast away with clenched, angry fists. At each visit, Olivia was on the brink of tears with ever-increasing frustration, while her mother marvelled at the fact that Rosie was not, shockingly enough, the world's best breastfeeder. Each time this happened, I suggested subtle changes to Olivia's positioning, becoming increasingly hands-on with every attempt until I finally took hold of the back of Rosie's shoulders myself, brushed her lips across Olivia's breast and moved her to the nipple with lightning speed when she finally opened her mouth wide enough to latch well. One suck, two sucks – and then Rosie grimaced, twisted her face away and fell asleep.

Olivia's mother observed these attempts with a knitted brow and a mouth that was pursed into a disapproving moue. 'I mean, I don't know what the issue is,' she said as I answered the buzzer for the umpteenth time. It was nearly six o'clock, and the air was heavy with the mingled odour of sweaty women and hospital dinners. 'Rosie's such a darling little thing, but poor Livvy can't seem to get the hang of it.'

I looked at Olivia. She had barely moved from the bed all day: her glossy hair was now frizzed with the heat of the ward, her make-up had begun to slide down her bloodless cheeks and even her breasts appeared to droop languidly between the open lapels of her pink pyjamas. This was a woman on the brink of a breakdown, and in her arms – squalling, squawking, downright pissed off – was a very hungry baby.

'Olivia,' I began, hoping the tone of my voice was just frank enough to initiate some plain-talking between us. 'What do you want to do?'

'She wants to breastfeed, of course!' replied her mother. I shot her a look: a cold, concentrated laser beam of midwife attitude. I didn't want to enter into a debate with her about her daughter's preferred feeding choices or the rights-or-wrongs of any of it. I knew that once I started, I wouldn't be able to stop. Not only that, I would probably allow my carefully crafted mask of calmness to slip, so strongly did I feel about Olivia's right to make her own decisions, and to deliver and feed her baby whatever the hell way she wanted to, or could.

'Olivia,' I repeated, ignoring her mother's interjection. 'What do *you* want to do? Whatever it is, I'll do everything I can to help you, but it has to be your call.'

Olivia looked up at me. Silently but steadily, streams of hot tears began to pour down her cheeks. There was no sobbing, no tearing of hair. She was too exhausted even for that. A long, futile labour, major abdominal surgery, three hours of sleep and the best part of a day's worth of jamming her breasts into her baby's angry, unyielding mouth had left Olivia completely and utterly spent.

'I do want to breastfeed,' she said, as the tears reached her jawline and trickled down her neck. 'I know Rosie's hungry. I've tried so hard. I just – I don't know what to do.'

I knelt down by Olivia, on the opposite side from her mother. 'Hey,' I said. 'We'll get this milk into your baby's tummy. It's OK if she's not latching right now. The main thing is that she gets fed. Do you know about hand-expressing?'

'You mean, milking myself? Like a cow?'

'Well, yes and no …' I replied. 'It might be a bit too soon to get you on the breast pump, but I can show you how to express the milk yourself into a pot, and then we can give it to Rosie in a little syringe. It takes a bit of getting used to, but it doesn't hurt.' I began flipping through the breastfeeding booklet I had left with Olivia, looking for the relevant illustrations.

On the other side of the bed, Olivia's mother clutched at her pearls in disgust. 'Really, now, there's no need for that kind of thing, is there? It's just so … crude.'

'It's the best way to keep the breasts stimulated for now,' I said, looking her dead in the eye. And then, to Olivia, 'Let's have a go.'

While Olivia's mother held Rosie (and very pointedly averted her eyes from the bed), I leaned over Olivia and talked her through the basic steps of hand-expressing, showing her how to grasp a handful of breast tissue and with long, steady squeezes, drizzle her milk into a sterile gallipot. The longer I held that awkward position, the more my hips and the backs of my thighs began to ache, compounded by the stair-climbing I'd squeezed in during my lunch break, in service to the Fat Bastards Club. It was worth the effort, though: within minutes, Olivia had mastered the technique and was squeezing jets of colostrum with one hand into the little tub she held in the other.

'Brilliant!' I said, slowly standing upright and feeling every vertebra in my spine stiffen as I did so. It was now almost seven o'clock, time to catch up with the day's documentation, write my part of the ward's evening report and do a quick walk-round to check that none of my other patients had fallen ill, had a nervous breakdown or absconded before I clocked off for the day. 'You've got loads of milk. Rosie's going to have a three-course meal,' I said as I tried to reverse discreetly out of the bed space. I took one last look as I backed away: Olivia, grappling bravely with her breasts as tears continued to slide down her face. Her mother, holding Rosie in a white-knuckled grip, pretending to study the abstract print of the curtain fabric while Olivia tried and tried to please them both. It was an image that returned to me as I drove home that evening, and again when I woke at two in the morning, unable to sleep. Olivia had stirred something in me, and as I lay there in the dark, counting the hours until the start of my third and final shift of the week, I shuddered with the memory of those early days of motherhood: the brain fog brought on by the relentless sleep deprivation and searing interludes of pain; the sudden and overwhelming rush of love for the baby, along with the dawning realisation that you will never, ever be able to do everything completely right for this child, no matter how hard you try. There is joy, yes, in that twilight haze of parenting, but underneath it all hums the guilt that drones at varying volumes through every woman's journey: I first heard that hum years ago as I lay in the hospital bed nursing a baby and a wound, and I heard it still as I slept fitfully that night in between shifts, wondering if I had done enough for Olivia and whether I would find her better – or broken – in the morning.

As it happened, when I drew back the curtain at the start of that third shift, I had to wonder whether the woman packing her bag with brisk efficiency was the same one who had nearly dissolved in a hot puddle of milk and tears the day before. Olivia was dressed, for one thing: the pink pyjamas had been replaced by a stylish jumper, skinny jeans and spotless white trainers. Her hair was slicked back in a high ponytail, and with a fresh shade of fuchsia lipstick, Olivia looked bright, healthy and put together. The scene was also notable for its lack of crying: at the bedside, Rosie lay serenely in her cot, wearing a lemon yellow sleepsuit with matching hat and mitts. What spoke loudest to me, though, was the empty chair in the corner: Olivia's mother was absent.

'Morning, Olivia!' I called from the foot of the bed. Olivia paused her packing and when she turned to face me, I could see that her eyes were tired, but there was a gentle softness to her features that had been missing among the previous day's dramas. 'Getting ready to go home?'

'Yes,' she said, and smiled. 'I finally managed to latch Rosie on overnight, and she's fed a few times already this morning. She kind of came on and off a bit, but we're getting there.'

'That's fantastic,' I said. 'I'm delighted for you. Sometimes it's easier to get the hang of things when your— when nobody's watching you.'

Olivia gave a wry laugh as she folded a stack of muslins and pressed them into the large duffel bag that lay open in front of her on the bed. 'You mean my mother. She's driving back home this morning. According to her, Dad can't even open his own Weetabix.'

'Well,' I ventured, 'she's quite a strong character.'

'Don't I know it. I did eighteen years of hard time in that house before I escaped to uni.' Olivia sighed as she placed a folded jumper into the bag.

'I guess mothers always want the best for their children,' I said, and as the words came out of my mouth, I knew I would never have been so charitable to Olivia's mother in person. There was something about that false, fixed grin that had made my bile rise. 'She just wants you to do things exactly the way she did, I suppose.'

'What do you mean?'

'Well, to have a vaginal birth, and then to breastfeed.'

Olivia tossed her ponytail back and laughed. 'Oh, I was born by C-section too!' she said. 'And she bottle-fed me and my brothers. She always said her milk never came in. She'll bore on about it for hours to anyone who asks.'

I was, quite literally, gobsmacked. I stood there with my mouth hanging open as Olivia crammed more clothes into her bag. Just as I had felt an overwhelming desire to help Olivia and to protect her from what I saw as her mother's overbearing passive-aggression, so I now felt a powerful and completely unexpected surge of sympathy – even sadness – for Olivia's mother. Here was a woman whose own birth experiences didn't go to her idealised plan, who tried and failed to breast-feed, who couldn't – despite her best efforts – do things the 'right' way, and was still projecting her hopes and sorrows onto her daughter a generation down the line. It's often said that women are their own worst enemies, a notion that can be confirmed by a single shift in a maternity hospital, where gossip and bullying often provide a bitter backing track to the overall thrum of kindness. Midwife to midwife, mother to daughter:

the gift of our love is so often tainted by our own guilt and sadness. Like the Fat Bastards climbing the stairs in pairs, only to descend and start again, each generation of women tries its best to brave the heights of motherhood, only for their daughters to begin again at the bottom with nothing but their mothers' dusty, weaving footprints as their guide.

'Could you give me a hand with this?' Olivia asked as she tugged at the zip on her bag, which was now stuffed to bursting. 'If you hold it at this end …'

I moved alongside her and as I grasped the bag where Olivia was pointing, I was met with my second surprise of the day. Inside, jammed into every available nook and cranny between jumpers, socks and Baby-gros, were at least a dozen bottles of ready-made formula. It wasn't unusual for formula-feeding mums to ask for a couple of bottles 'for the road', but this was a bit excessive, especially for a woman who had spent the previous day working her nipples to the nub in the name of breastfeeding.

'I'll pull the zip if you can grab the side,' Olivia suggested, oblivious to my discovery.

As Olivia wrestled with the bag, I wrestled with my thoughts. It would have been easy to zip it all up and send Olivia on her way without comment – after all, she'd had enough 'helpful' hints from her mother – but the temptation was too strong.

'Wow,' I said. 'That's a lot of milk.'

Olivia straightened up and looked me squarely in the eye. 'Just in case,' she said. Her gaze was firm – every bit as steely as her mother's – as if silently daring me to reply.

I tightened my grip, she grabbed the zip, and together we closed the bag.

Notes on Triage

'Triage, Midwife Hazard speaking, how can I help you?'

'I think everyone in my office can smell my vagina.'

'My husband left the heating on all night and now I'm really thirsty.'

'I'm at the departure gate in the airport, can you tell the ground crew I'm fit to fly?'

'If I go blonde, will it hurt my baby?'

'If I put olive oil in my ear, will it hurt my baby?'

'My baby hasn't moved in the last twenty minutes.'

'My baby hasn't moved in three hours.'

'My baby hasn't moved since yesterday.'

'I'm bleeding.'

'I'm pushing.'

'I can feel something coming out.'

'The baby is here.'

When I tell people that I'm a midwife, I tend to get one of two responses: 1) It must be so amazing to deliver babies all day long; and 2) it must be so nice to cuddle babies all day long. Yes, some lucky midwives on the postnatal ward do occasionally cuddle babies, although these rare, cosy moments are little recompense for the rest of the working day and the mountains of documentation required to get these newborns and their mothers out the door on the hallowed day of discharge. Births and baby cuddles apart, most midwives in the NHS are actually engaged in caring for women in the nine months leading up to delivery (and for up to six weeks afterwards). Early pregnancy units, outpatient clinics, day-care suites, antenatal wards – all are devoted to nurturing pregnancies safely from a tiny cluster of cells to a bawling bundle of joy. Anything and everything can and does go wrong during that 'magical' journey, and while Mrs Celeb is blooming on the cover of *OK!* magazine, showcasing her perfectly airbrushed bump in a birth pool made of Carrara marble and unicorn sparkles, most mere mortals are busy bleeding, aching, cramping, or generally stressing out in a pair of baggy maternity leggings passed down from Auntie Senga after she had her twins in 1997.

Of course, while every woman is offered regular antenatal check-ups and postnatal visits, there's an awful lot of bleeding/stressing/googling going on in between times. But fear not, the NHS in all of its wondrous foresight has gifted the women of Britain a repository for all of their out-of-hours hopes, dreams and worries: Maternity Triage (aptly named in a grim nod to the battlefield). It was here that I settled, having completed my clinical rotation through almost all of the different wards and areas in which you'll find a midwife. When I first encountered the department, I was overwhelmed by its relentless pace and head-spinning variety, terrified by the seemingly endless drama. In time, though, this was the very quality that drew me back again and again and I eventually became acquainted with the full spectrum of dilemmas and disasters that can afflict the pregnant populace day or night. As I gained experience and confidence, the complex cases that had once brought me out in a cold sweat gradually became fascinating problems to be unravelled and solved as part of a dynamic team. The cocktail of clinical challenge, adrenaline and dark humour became intoxicating and addictive.

I often describe Triage to family, friends and inquisitive hairdressers as 'Accident & Emergency for pregnant people'. However, unlike an A&E nurse, whose most urgent patients have already been filtered by a far-off call handler, the Triage midwife has the joy of fielding all of the panicked phone calls as well as the face-to-face emergencies. Although women are briefed at the start of their pregnancy to use the twenty-four-hour Triage hotline for serious concerns only, the concept of 'serious' is highly subjective. While one woman may resist phoning the hospital until she is actually hosing blood across the lino, there are another ten women who will speed-dial Triage because some faceless online 'friend' has warned them that one lick of a Mr Whippy ice cream can cause instant fetal distress. (To save you the Google time – it won't.) A woman who's worried that bleaching her roots might kill her baby can be tying up the phone lines while another woman across town is trying to get through with a question about the sizeable clot she's just passed down the toilet. A single shift in Triage, or even an hour on the phones, can take a midwife from the ridiculous to the sublime and back again. As a wise midwife once said, it's no wonder we drink.

Hawa:
Word Medicine and the
Pee Baby

A wet Wednesday morning in November, and morale in the hospital was ...

Well, I could say 'at a low ebb', but the word 'ebb' suggests a wave lapping gently at a velvet-sanded shore. In reality, it felt as though a giant sinkhole had opened in the middle of the Atlantic and sucked every drop of the world's joy into its black, churning vortex. No one in a uniform was immune; even my own usually cheery disposition had morphed into a demeanour of brooding disgruntlement, punctuated by the occasional scowl.

Maternity services do tend to undergo a natural rise and fall in activity, with one week being relatively quiet, while the next week bears the busy fruit of some event that happened nine months before – a snowstorm, perhaps, or a spell of warm weather, or even a particularly bad week of telly. September is a consistently hectic time for us, as all those messy Christmas parties and snogs under the mistletoe materialise into wards brimming with bawling babies. This peak season of births is almost comfortingly consistent, proving to midwives year upon year that yes, an extra glass of Prosecco and a Santa hat are really all it takes to get human beings to breed.

However, sometimes there is a sudden spike in the birth rate with no apparent reason or warning, and so it was that November. Labourer after labourer came careering into Triage, practically skidding through the doors on a slippery stream of amniotic fluid, and no sooner had each woman been examined than she was trundled onto the nearest bed or wheelchair and rushed up to the labour ward. Over and over again, we made the same call to the labour ward sister, phone clenched between chin and shoulder, hands still gloved and ready: 'I've got a para two at fully.' 'I've got a prim at nine centimetres.' 'I've got a woman here – I don't know her name, but she's pushing.' As the month wore on, each phone call was met with increasing levels of exasperation (and increasingly creative expletives). 'I don't have a free midwife,' came the reply. 'I don't have any clean rooms.' 'Just deliver her.' 'Deliver her.' 'Deliver her.'

The baby boom couldn't have come at a worse time. One lot of junior doctors had recently left to start their next placements, fanning out across the city to the fresh pastures of dermatology, neurology and the psychiatric ward, and a new group of bright-eyed twelve-year-olds (or so they often appeared) had arrived to take their places. Some of them were remarkably competent, having come from rotations in A&E with its pick-and-mix of crash calls and medical mysteries, but many of them were quite clearly terrified by the challenge of being the responsible medic in an acute environment for the first time. To make matters worse, many of the young male doctors appeared to have only ever seen naked women in their textbooks, and these poor chaps could hardly conceal their terror when presented with the real thing. Breasts swollen and hard with mastitis were approached with shaking hands, speculums were nervously squeezed into vaginas the wrong way round, and God help the virginal male trainee who comes face-to-face with his first Brazilian bikini wax under the watchful eye of a chaperoning midwife. Many a time have I had to pull a new doctor aside and remind him that he needs to wash his hands, introduce himself, and make eye contact with a patient before making contact with her vagina.

The pressures of the system were hard enough to bear for the staff who had worked within its confines for years, but for the thinner-skinned among us, it was hell. I had entered midwifery with the hope of providing unhurried, compassionate care, and as the hospital groaned under the weight of its workload, that goal became virtually impossible to achieve. Days and nights merged into one frantic blur. By the end of each shift, I had only a vague memory of the names and histories of the women I'd encountered at its beginning. Some of my senior colleagues charged blithely through this onslaught, gimlet-eyed and undeterred, and while I tried hard to follow their example, I couldn't help feeling increasingly like a worn cog in a giant machine. I had the uneasy sensation that I was simply processing women, not caring for them, and the feeling didn't sit well with my soul.

On that November morning, I had just thrown on my uniform and was mentally girding myself for the day ahead when I heard what sounded like a baby's hungry cry coming from the corner of the changing rooms. My heart flip-flopped in my chest and I froze on the spot, contemplating what kind of monumental screw-up could have landed an unattended newborn in the staff area. Midwifery is full of these paradoxical moments: on the one hand, you've seen so much strangeness that nothing surprises you any more; on the other hand, the wonderful world of womankind continues to throw ever crazier business your way. The cry started again, softer this time, and I crept past rows of lockers until I located its source.

A young midwife sat on the far end of a bench, head bowed, weeping. I had met Trisha briefly on several occasions. She had rotated through the wards as a student, and had only recently finished her training and qualified, a couple of years after I'd done it myself. She was one of those idealistic and almost naively brave young women who had gone straight from secondary school to midwifery, and I recalled that in my few interactions with her, she had been shy but diligent, and kind to the patients in her care.

I approached her the way you might approach an injured animal: gently, eyes down, a little bit sideways so as to appear as unthreatening as possible. Crouching at her feet, I could see that her face was scarlet and raw, with tears tracking slowly down her neck and collecting in a damp ring around the collar of her uniform. It was 7.26 a.m. – nearly time for both of us to start our shifts – but she looked like she'd been crying for hours.

'Trisha?' I said. She rubbed her fists in her eyes and looked up at me from under a cloud of auburn hair.

'I'm sorry,' she said. 'I'm so embarrassed. I'm fine, really. Go ahead.'

'Can I do anything for you?'

'It's just … I can't do it any more. I can't face it. Even walking into the building in the morning, I want to …' She hiccupped, chest heaving. 'I want to scream and run away. My heart starts racing before I've even got to the labour ward. It's so hard not knowing what the day will bring.'

I looked at Trisha, then down at the floor. 'We all feel like that,' I replied.

'I know,' she said, sobbing. 'It's so bad that I – I mean, I'm usually a calm person, but I – I haven't been sleeping, and I've been having nightmares about women dying, and babies dying, and I pull the buzzer for help and nobody comes.' This story was all too familiar. Recently, the anxiety of the job had become so all-encompassing that, like many of my colleagues, I'd been having increasingly frequent and vivid nightmares about obstetric emergencies. For the midwife with an unmanageable workload, each sleep brings fresh horror, and when it's not your patient who's in trouble, it's you – delivering your own baby in an unfamiliar room, on a bus, or in a park, no help in sight, blood running down your legs and a feeling of being completely, terribly alone. You wake with your pulse racing, dreading the beep of your alarm, knowing that in a few short hours you'll be at another bedside, pretending to be in control.

Trisha sniffed and wiped her nose with the back of her hand. 'When I finally told Sister how bad it was, and that I'd been to the GP and he'd put me on antidepressants, she just laughed and said, that's fine, because pretty much everyone else in here is on them already.' At that, a fresh wave of tears sprang forth, and Trisha buried her face in her hands again.

I remembered reading about an American lay midwife called Sister Morningstar – a half-Cherokee, self-proclaimed 'mystic' who lived in the Ozark Mountains – who wrote of herbal poultices, and ancient birthways, and the judicious use of what she called 'word medicine' to empower and heal the women who sought her guidance. I often thought of Sister Morningstar when confronted by a patient whose emotional turmoil far outweighed any physical concern. In these cases, I had found, a carefully crafted consolation or encouragement could completely transform the patient's experience. Although words often come to me more easily on paper than they do to my tongue, I had come to appreciate 'word medicine' as a crucial element of the midwife's craft.

I looked at Trisha and wished I had the right words to heal her condition, but the truth was, I had often felt as she did: the gut-clenching anxiety, the dread of what was to come, the humiliation when your superiors smell your fear and dismiss it. Already, in the short, sharp shock of my first few years as a midwife, I had learned that the only cure for this despair was a kind of brutal exposure therapy: you keep turning up, shift after shift, and you endure it, and you internalise it, and one day you find that you've traded fear for numbness. It is that numbness that enables you to grind away, day after day – but at what cost?

'Trisha,' I began. 'The fact that you're even here shows that you have a bigger pair of balls than most people out in the world. You chose to do this, and you're doing it. Think of all the women you've helped already in your three years of being a student, and then in the months since you've been qualified. You've delivered how many babies?'

Trisha gazed at the floor. 'Eighty-two.'

'There you go. Eighty-two lives you've brought into the world. Pretty freaking amazing, if you ask me. And you could have worked in a shop, or in a bank, or whatever, but you chose to do this, and be here.'

Trisha lifted her head, smoothed her hair away from her face, and looked at me squarely. 'Well, I'm not doing it any more.' Her eyes were still bleary but her voice suddenly had a steely edge. 'I can't live like this. I can't do this for the next forty years, or fifty years, or whenever they decide I can finally get my pension. Twelve-hour night shifts when I'm sixty-eight? You've got to be kidding me.' She drew herself up, her spine lengthening as her decision was made. 'I. Just. Can't.' And then, in one swift movement of unwavering intention, she picked up her bag, pulled her jacket from her locker, walked past me, and left the hospital.

What was there to say? What 'word medicine', if any, could have altered that outcome? How can you triage burnout? Trisha wasn't the first midwife to down tools – in fact, she was the third midwife that month – and she certainly wouldn't be the last. There are times when a kind word or stern pep talk can bring a midwife back from the edge – on any given shift, you will find us gathered in whispering clusters for exactly this purpose, huddled in the storeroom among a forest of drip stands, or hiding in the no-man's land between theatres and the sluice – but Trisha was already well beyond the point of comfort or persuasion. Watching her hunched figure disappear out the door, I had something akin to an out-of-body experience; part of me remained rooted to the spot, but another seemed to slip all too easily into Trisha's skin. As I had done so many times since that first night shift as a student, I felt the lure of the car park, the blast of fresh air and the cool kiss of drizzle on my cheeks as I stepped outside, the ease with which I could drive away and melt into the anonymity of the morning rush hour. Normal people were out there, doing normal things – changing the radio station on a dashboard, tightening the straps on a child's schoolbag, pushing a trolley around a quiet supermarket – and I could choose to move among them, as Trisha had chosen. That urge to retreat had welled up again and again over the years, and at times the pull had almost been stronger than my sense of obligation to the women in my care. Only a nudge from a colleague – or, more often, the shameful prospect of having to explain my cowardice to family and friends – had propelled me through those other doors to the main hospital corridor and the work that lay beyond.

It was 7.32 and I was now late for my shift. I ran to Triage, trainers smacking off the freshly buffed floor, badges and fob watch flapping noisily on my chest. When I arrived at the desk, it was clear that the day's tsunami of babies was already in full flow: both phones were ringing, there were three names on the board, and four women in various stages of labour – and degrees of distress – were pacing the waiting-room floor.

Stephanie, the other midwife on that day's shift, appeared at the threshold to the main treatment area. Only twenty-six years old, she too had hurtled head-long into midwifery straight from school, but Stephanie was one of the lucky ones who seemed unfazed by anything this place could throw at her. Her heart was soft but her confident exterior was unshakeable even in the most acute scenarios, and her language was unremittingly, fantastically filthy. White plastic apron tied tightly around her waist, gloved hands planted firmly on her hips, she was a formidable figure.

'All right, Steph?'

She stuck out her bottom lip and blew her fringe away from her face. 'Piss and shit!' she exclaimed as her fringe fell right back into place.

'What's happening?'

'No, seriously, it's piss and shit. Bed two hasn't taken a dump in eight days, one of the side rooms is shitting for Britain and has probably given everyone in the waiting room a dose of C. diff, and the one in bed four … she's all yours, hot lips.'

'Piss?' I said, nodding towards that bed space.

'Correctamundo', said Stephanie, breezing past me towards the phone at the desk. 'How's your catheter-isation these days?' she called over her shoulder.

'Pretty sweet,' I replied, which – if you will allow me to blow my own single-use-only, gently lubricated trumpet – is actually true. These days, I reckon I could probably whack in a catheter whilst blindfolded, in a wind tunnel, with my teeth. Unlikely, I know, but should such a clinical situation ever arise, I'm your woman.

It has not always been thus. As a student, catheterisation was a skill that eluded me, in spite of many kind, forgiving women who pretended not to mind when I missed my target and catheterised their vagina for the umpteenth time. The more I failed, the more I was determined to succeed, as catheterisation is such a useful, albeit unglamorous, skill. It's essential for women with epidural anaesthetics, for those with bladder trauma, and for any patient whose perineum is such a mess that it's kinder not to force her to wee directly on her stitches for a day or so after birth. The ability to pass a little plastic tube into a lady's waterworks may not be sexy, but to paraphrase cinematic anchorman Ron Burgundy, it's kind of a big deal.

What can be so challenging about this simple task? you ask. Dear reader, without putting too fine a point on it, sometimes just locating a woman's urethra can be like finding a needle in a fleshy haystack. Contrary to a belief still widely held by a surprisingly large proportion of the general public, women don't have 'one big hole' down there, some kind of universal two-way chute for babies, urine, penises and the odd light bulb (yes, it happens, and no, I don't recommend it). Indeed, if you're a female reader and this is the first you've heard of this anatomical complexity, I encourage you to spend some quality time with your vulva and a mirror.

My first successful catheterisation was performed on a night shift halfway through the second year of my training. The room was warm and dimly lit, and I gazed hopefully into the eyes of my patient, who was six centimetres dilated and had an epidural so effective that you could have driven a team of wild horses through her vagina and she would barely have flinched. I opened the necessary packs, being careful to keep an aseptic field as I had been taught, and shone a spotlight on my target. The whole procedure went like clockwork, my patient remained supremely comfortable, and I could actually have kissed her when I saw the flashback of golden fluid start to rush through the catheter tubing. I was so delighted with myself that I remained perched on the edge of the bed for a few more minutes, lecturing the patient in worldly-wise tones about my plans to guide her through the next stage of her labour, when I realised that a warm wetness was seeping through my scrubs. I soon realised that I had forgotten to close the tap that sealed the urine collection bag on the end of the catheter, and while I had been dazzling my patient with my clinical brilliance, I had also soaked myself from waist to toe in her urine. My mentor, silently bouncing on a birth ball in the corner of the room, had observed the whole sorry scene and said not a word until I realised my mistake. She did allow me to change my scrubs, knowing full well that I would need to access the changing room via the desk and the bunker, where all of the other midwives, auxiliaries and theatre staff could enjoy the sight of the piss-soaked student. Midwifery Lesson Number 156: always close the catheter tap. (See also Midwifery Lesson Number 157: always bring a spare pair of pants to work.)

Fast-forward to that sodden Wednesday a few years later, by which time I had learned these, and many other, valuable lessons. Having left the labour ward, the opportunities to catheterise Triage patients were few and far between, so I picked up bed four's notes and read them with interest. Hawa was a twenty-one-year-old Somali woman who had recently been granted leave to remain in the UK, and was forty weeks and two days pregnant with her first child. Rifling through her paperwork, it seemed that Hawa's pregnancy had been fairly unremarkable: a bit of early nausea, then a scare with a small bleed at twenty weeks, then routine antenatal appointments and a plan for induction of labour at forty-two weeks. No history of urinary issues, and the call sheet clipped to the front of the case notes read simply, *Abdo pain, patient unsure when she last passed urine, query labour.*

I pulled back the curtain around bed four. A woman in a long purple nightie was on all fours on the bed, bottom raised towards me, head down, a thousand tight black braids spilling out onto the starched white pillow. A hijab had been neatly folded over the chair by the bedside; like many of the devout women I had encountered, Hawa had swapped a degree of modesty for comfort as soon as she was safely ensconced in the female sanctuary of Triage.

'Hawa?' I asked, and the woman whipped her braids back and smiled at me over her shoulder. She was beautiful, with flawless amber skin stretched over the highest, most regal cheekbones, and a long, graceful neck.

'Sorry, sorry,' she said as she turned round to face me. 'I was trying to get comfortable. The pain is very bad.' Although her smile didn't waver, I heard the coarse crack in her voice. 'It has been worse since this morning.'

'Is the pain there all the time, or does it come and go in waves?' I asked, thinking that at this point in her baby's gestation, Hawa was most likely to be experiencing the crampy tightenings of early labour.

'It's there all the time,' she said, 'all across here,' and she moved her hands over her belly, long fingers tracing the pain.

'And when did you last pass urine?'

'This is the thing. I'm not sure. I – I can't remember. My husband thinks maybe last night. He wanted to come here but I said don't be silly, it's nothing, go to work. His boss, he is very strict, he does not like lateness.' She smiled again, but her fingers grasped a little tighter at the purple fabric of her gown.

Moving to the bedside, I asked Hawa if she would mind drawing up her nightie so that I could have a feel of her abdomen. Palpation is the first step in many antenatal examinations, as it tells the midwife so much: how large the uterus is, whether the baby is well grown, which way the baby is facing, and whether the muscles are soft and relaxed, or taut with contractions, or rigid with a hidden bleed. I reached for a sheet to cover Hawa's legs – we do try to preserve patients' modesty, in spite of the commonly accepted notion that pregnancy requires women to 'check your dignity at the door' – but as Hawa lifted her gown, cold panic glued me to the spot. Instead of being smooth and round, Hawa's bump looked like a water balloon that had been cinched in the middle with a tight belt.

My face must have betrayed my surprise as my hands traced the indentation across Hawa's midline. 'Is everything all right?' she asked, eyes widening.

Bandl's ring, I thought. *It's unmistakeable.* A rarely seen sign of a dangerously obstructed labour, this invisible drawstring around a woman's abdomen was something I had only read about, but here was one in real life. Maybe Hawa had been contracting for days without realising it, and for whatever reason the baby's passage through the pelvis had been blocked, and this fibrous ring had begun its deadly constriction who knows how many hours ago.

'I just need to have more of a feel,' I stalled, and my hands moved lower down Hawa's abdomen. As I felt the telltale bulge of a grossly distended bladder, I began to second-guess myself. Could this be the true cause of Hawa's bizarre shape? I strapped the fetal monitor to her belly and the baby's heartbeat ticked loud and steady. *Fetal heart 140 beats per minute*, I thought, planning my notes as the monitor drummed on. *Accelerations present, no decelerations*. Beyond the curtain, five other babies' heartbeats chugged away in interweaving rhythm. The room was busying up – Stephanie's voice was somewhere to my left, advising a woman to 'breathe, don't push, just breathe breathe breathe' followed by the squeal of wheels against linoleum as another bed was dragged towards the door.

'I think your baby sounds fine,' I said to Hawa as the monitor continued its steady beat, 'but I'm not sure what to think about the shape of your bump. Do you really think that maybe you haven't peed since yesterday?'

Hawa rubbed her belly. 'I think yes, this may be true. I have been up since very early this morning, and yes – maybe – perhaps it was the afternoon when I last passed water.'

I studied the trace of the baby's heartbeat, which still looked completely normal, with no sign of the potentially fatal distress that a Bandl's ring would cause. *Cool your jets*, I said to myself. *You could page the doctor for an emergency that isn't really there, or you could catheterise and see if a good, long pee makes this bulge disappear.* As the thunderous chorus of heartbeats all around me seemed to grow louder, my decision was made for me. *Just get on with it,* I thought. *If she does have a ring, then you freak out, page the medics, and stand back while the faeces hits the fan. But not before.*

Hawa wasn't wild about the idea of being catheterised (because really, who *is?* It's a bit of a niche interest), but the pain in her abdomen was becoming so intense that the possibility of swift relief was too attractive to refuse. As soon as she consented, my panic receded. I was back on familiar ground, retrieving the necessary pack from the bedside trolley, pulling the corners open with care as if it were the most wonderful Christmas present, each component nestled in the crisp white paper, a neat-freak midwife's dream. I splashed some sterile water into a little tub, pulled my gloves on with a satisfying smack, and prepared myself for a nifty bit of catheterisation while Hawa drew her legs up.

And there it was. Another shockwave that made my heart turn over in my chest, but this time, the shock was tempered with sadness as I realised what I was seeing, and the true cause of Hawa's pain revealed itself.

While every woman's genitalia are different, with variations in size, texture and proportion, we all share a basic structure, and there is actually a comforting truth to the cliché that once you've seen one vulva, you've seen them all. However, what Hawa was showing me was not what nature had gifted her: even an untrained eye could have seen that this was something that had been cut, reshaped and sewn back together, most probably many years ago, most likely in a faraway place. Where I expected to see soft, fleshy folds, there was a smooth surface, like the sexless Barbie dolls I used to collect as a child. The edges of Hawa's skin had been brought together to create a small, crudely fashioned opening, and even with my sharply angled torch, I could only just see where my catheter needed to go. As I probed gently with gloved fingers, I confirmed that Hawa was one of the increasing number of women we'd been seeing who had been cut as a child. Most of these women were from countries where the practice of cutting young women and girls in various intimate ways was a centuries-old tradition. While this mutilation and desexualisation are undoubtedly horrific, it's difficult for midwives, politicians or anyone responsible for women's safety to know how best to approach the issue with sensitivity: the practice of Female Genital Mutilation (FGM) may be rooted in only the most tenuous religious doctrine, but many parents and elders perform FGM in the mistaken belief that it will preserve their daughters' virtue and, by extension, the family's honour. What is criminal in one country can be seen as sacred in another, no matter how brutal the act.

Swallowing down my anger at whatever long-ago auntie or neighbour had done this to Hawa, I continued my work, passing the slender tube where it needed to go and watching with relief as urine began to rush out. The collection bag at the end of the tube began to fill, and it wasn't long until there was almost a litre of fluid inside it. Clearly, the pressure of a fully grown baby had been too much for Hawa's altered anatomy to handle, and her bladder had simply backed up. It was possible, even likely, that Hawa had endured years of urinary and sexual dysfunction, but like so many women in her situation, shame had stopped her from disclosing her history. Living with this secret, she had not sought any kind of medical treatment until today's pain required her to do so.

I looked up to Hawa's belly. As the catheter bag filled, I could actually see the bulge in her lower abdomen disappear and, as it did so, her bump evened out as I watched, settling into the smooth, round shape it should have had from the start.

I must have been too quiet for a little too long. Hawa looked down the bed questioningly, but my usual midwife patter failed me. For the second time that morning, I was lost for words. Where to begin? What was the right 'word medicine' for this beautiful woman who had crossed continents to end up on this bed, wholly reliant on me at that moment to keep her and her baby safe? Now that I knew Hawa had been cut, I was obliged by law and hospital protocol to ask her how, and when, and where, and to get her reviewed by the doctor, and to link her in to a gynaecological follow-up plan that might slowly reverse the pain and dysfunction she had probably been suffering for years. If her baby was a girl, Hawa would face fresh questioning and surveillance to ensure that her child wouldn't fall victim to the same fate, but there was no guarantee that the cycle would stop. The law is strong, but sometimes the pull of tradition is stronger.

'Is it OK?' Hawa asked, nervously pulling at the rumpled purple fabric of her gown.

So I did what midwives do. I took a deep breath, and I smiled. Gently, I lifted the catheter bag off the bed, cradling it in my arms. It had the warm, soft heft of a newborn, and I lifted it so Hawa could see. 'Congratulations,' I replied, grinning. 'We've delivered your pee baby. Now we just have to deliver the one in here,' I said, nodding to Hawa's belly.

She looked at me, then she looked at the sloshing, golden bundle in my arms, and she laughed. Slender neck thrown back, eyes closed, braids dancing around her head, she laughed until she shook, and I laughed with her. And we sat there laughing together, while her baby's heartbeat drummed steadily around us, until we stilled and gasped for breath.

Notes on Getting It Wrong

Mistakes will be made.

Children will write their name backwards. Cashiers will hand back the wrong change. Drivers will run red lights. And midwives will get stuff wrong, along with doctors, nurses, dentists, firefighters, teachers, police officers and pretty much everyone else who gets paid by the public to get stuff right.

It's a design flaw; people are prone to glitches – neurons firing gaily in the wrong direction, lighting up the brain like a pinball machine gone haywire – especially in times of extreme physical or emotional stress. Unfortunately, I slept through my alarm on the day when my midwifery tutor gave the lecture on How Not to Be Human; consequently, I am prone to all of the same foibles as the rest of the population. Most of the time, these errors have zero impact on my patients: I spell 'intravenous' wrong, I spill my coffee, I get halfway through my shift before clutching my unusually soft, free-flapping breasts in horror and realising that I forgot to put my bra on that morning.

Sometimes, though, my innate human knack for howling self-sabotage really comes to the fore, and I just plain get stuff wrong. There was the time when I misjudged the speed of a patient's labour. She was a first-time mother who sauntered quite casually up to the Triage desk, barely flinched at a vaginal examination which revealed her to be six centimetres dilated, and then proceeded to push out a baby in the middle of a busy corridor as I oh-so-casually walked her along to the labour ward lifts, believing, until the moment I saw that telltale, baby-shaped bulge in her sweatpants, that we had all the time in the world. There was also that other time when, to the great and lasting hilarity of my colleagues, I spent twenty minutes on the phone talking a woman through what seemed to be the throes of advanced labour, only to be told by the paramedics who grudgingly brought her to hospital that the patient was, in fact, only five months pregnant, and felt so much better after doing a giant poo. As a student, these kinds of mistakes are mortifying, especially when they're broadcast to the rest of the shift's staff with great embellishment. Time, age and experience eventually smooth the edges of that piercing shame and as long as no significant harm is done, the canny midwife knows to suck up these glitches, learn from them and even accept them as an inevitable part of the job.

Fortunately (or not, depending on how you look at it), I'm not the only clinician ever to have made an error of judgement; the long hours, the scant resources, the constant emotional strain and the notoriously unpredictable workings of the body might have something to do with the prevalence of human error in the health services. Sometimes the mistakes midwives make actually have very little to do with birth, and more to do with the myriad of medical conditions that can be triggered or exacerbated by pregnancy. This is the real 'meat' of Triage. Yes, our patients have uteruses (uteri? I've never been comfortable with that pompous plural), but they also have all of the other organs that non-pregnant people possess – the soft, fleshy baggage that makes us all human. These organs, from liver to lungs, from kidneys to colon, can backfire in spectacular fashion, leading to confusion, consternation and yes, mistakes.

As midwives, we develop an intricate understanding of pregnant physiology and all of its potential problems, but when complex medical conditions intersect with obstetrics, our partnership with doctors comes into its own. We may slate the young ones for their wide-eyed enthusiasm, bemoan the sneaky ones who demonstrate selective deafness when their pagers go off, and formulate personal lists of the ones we'd never, *ever* let near our sisters and daughters, but the good ones – the ones who listen, who collaborate, who learn and teach in equal measure, who possess that perfect combination of knowledge and creativity – these are the ones we want by the bedside when a pregnant woman gets really, really sick. We love these doctors. We bring them tea and biscuits when they're on the verge of collapse after five straight hours in theatre. We nod sympathetically when they tell us they can't remember the last time they saw their children in daylight. And we may or may not cut their hair in the middle of Triage on a rare quiet night shift.

I had a high-school biology teacher with a syrupy Southern accent and a wry sense of humour who enjoyed strolling among the lab benches as his hapless students struggled over dissections and diagrams. 'Weeeell,' he would drawl as he stopped by one particularly flummoxed pair of lab partners, 'two half-wits make a whole-wit.'

I often hear Mr Combs's voice in my head amid the din of Triage, especially when presenting a doctor with a case history that's got me stumped. With years of training but often precious few hours of sleep between us, we discuss, debate, and finally we hatch a plan. Sometimes one or both of us gets it wrong, and mistakes will be made, but every now and then our two half-baked halfwits come together, and eventually, blessedly, just-in-the-nick-of-time-edly, we get it right.

Tina:
Flu Season and Fear

'Did you bring a sample?'

'Yes, it's just here.'

She reached into her bag, withdrew the red-capped vial of golden liquid, and passed it to me with a smile.

This is the ritual of the antenatal clinic: the Patient, knowing she will be called upon to present a urine sample, gives the hallowed jar to the Oracle. The Oracle, in return, plunges her sacred, divining dipstick into the fluid – once, twice, three times in solemn succession – reads the colours blooming in tiny squares now along the length of the stick, and pronounces her wisdom.

'You have protein in your urine.'

'You've got an infection brewing.'

'There's glucose here,' she may say gravely. 'Is there any family history of diabetes?'

'No,' the patient replies. 'But I did have two bowls of Frosties, a chocolate chip muffin and a cappuccino with three sugars before I came here today.'

And thus it was spoken on that Monday morning in December, when I had been 'pulled' from my usual home in Triage to help out in the antenatal clinic along the corridor. Staff from every ward had been shuffled and redistributed across the hospital like a pack of cornflower-blue cards, and instead of answering the day's first phone calls about leaky vaginas and babies who won't move, I had been hustled into a small, unfamiliar room, armed only with a blood-pressure cuff, a Sonicaid and a drawer full of leaflets about pelvic pain. The unit had been short-staffed overnight, I was told, and apparently it was to be short-staffed again for that day, and the next, and the next. 'Flu season,' the night staff had groaned by way of explanation before flapping out the door in hastily donned winter coats and scarves, hurrying off to scrape their icy windscreens before heading for home and bed.

In addition to the ever-exciting game of 'Musical Chairs for Midwives', flu season brings with it a raft of delights including the Peer Vaccination Programme (a cheery diversion which requires the dutiful midwife to spend her lunch break seeking out a colleague willing to inject her with that season's flu vaccine in the cosy confines of the drugs cupboard), and also the famous Flu-Like Symptoms (a fantastically vague, catch-all term that can refer to sniffles, sneezes, sore throats, feeling hot, feeling cold, nausea, diarrhoea, aches, generalised malaise, and pretty much every other condition that might affect the average human on any given morning in the middle of winter).

That being said, midwives themselves have actually developed a very specific and highly accurate way of diagnosing flu: 'There could be a tenner on the ground next to you,' as one colleague put it, 'and you wouldn't even have the energy to drag yourself off the couch and pick it up.' This is a pretty clear-cut diagnostic tool for the averagely hard-up midwife, whose wages have slid so much in real terms over the past few years that a spare tenner would normally prompt a mirac- ulous, Lazarus-like recovery. Differentiating your 'worried well' pregnant woman from the genuinely sick patient can be less straightforward, however, and any midwife runs the daily risk of Getting It Wrong. Given the sheer volume of women who phone and attend the unit during every shift, and the inescapable fact that midwives are (I've said it once, but to drill home the truth of it, I'll say it again) only human, there is a small but inevitable group of patients whose concerns will be dismissed, misdiagnosed or mismanaged.

That morning, it seemed as though every patient attending their routine appointments in the antenatal clinic had flu-like symptoms, and although I'd satisfied myself that there was nothing seriously wrong with the five patients I'd seen so far, I'd also drained the bottle of hand gel on my desk after being sneezed on, sniffled at and sprayed with five different flavours of mucus. I was gazing at the computer screen, waiting for the online records system to muddle through its own winter fug and rubbing my red-raw hands absent-mindedly, when the clinic's clerkess popped her face round the door.

'Your last patient is here,' she said. Her lips twitched as if she were trying to suppress a giggle.

I looked up from the computer. It was unusual for the clerkess to come and announce a patient; the waiting room was full of women in various stages of pregnancy, boredom and frustration – you just had to grab a set of case notes from the pile by the wall, call out a name, and one of the crowd would follow you dutifully to your room.

'OK, thanks for that,' I replied with a brief smile, looking back at the computer.

The clerkess hovered inexplicably by the door. 'And she's wearing a dog lead,' she said with unconcealed delight, as she tossed a thick blue file onto the desk and disappeared back into the throng of the waiting room.

Well, I thought as I sat back in my chair, *if that's what you're into* ... At one time or another, I had looked after women with all kinds of personal proclivities and a patient in full bondage gear – dog lead, leather mask, the lot – would hardly have surprised me. In fact, that kind of get-up would be a bit vanilla compared to some of the stories I'd heard in the staff room. *Never mind*, I thought, as I pulled the case notes towards me on the desk. *Let's see what you're up to ... Justyna.* I flipped open the notes and scanned the documentation inside: she was a twenty-nine-week primigravida with a history of cardiac surgery as an infant, but nothing remarkable since then. She'd recently been to the ultrasound department for a scan, which had shown a well-grown baby and a placenta in the right place. All pretty standard. I glanced at my fob watch as I rose from the desk; it was 12.46, and with any luck I could finish Justyna's appointment quickly and bolt down some lunch before heading back to Triage for the usual afternoon rush.

There were still a few stragglers in the waiting room – rosy-cheeked women of various gestations, rifling through the piles of well-thumbed magazines that had been donated to the department many moons ago – but there was only one woman wearing a dog lead. I realised when I saw her that the clerkess had used the word 'wearing' for dramatic effect: the lead, a length of muddy yellow cord, was actually draped around Justyna's shoulders. Given the fact that she also wore a knee-length down jacket and a battered old pair of wellington boots, I surmised that my patient had come directly from the park or the woods to the hospital. Perhaps she'd been in too much of a rush to realise that the lead was round her neck, or that her mop of black curls was crowned with brambly twigs. It was a marvel she didn't have a Labrador with her to complete the picture. *Dragged through an actual hedge backwards*, I thought to myself, and then called out loud, 'Justyna?'

Nobody looked up. Had I got it wrong? Certainly, there was only one woman wearing a dog lead – I scanned the room again to be sure. The woman who I presumed to be Justyna was gazing intently at the floor, wild hair obscuring her face. 'Justyna?' I called again in her direction, louder this time.

The other ladies glanced at each other and returned to their magazines. There was a long pause, and then slowly, painstakingly, as if every incremental movement was causing the vertebrae in her neck to crumble with the effort, Justyna lifted her head and fixed me with a hollow stare, the blackness of her pupils appearing to recede into a void deep within her head. Her cheeks were drawn, her lips pale and tight. She coughed – a deep, rattling hack – and pressed her eyelids closed as a shiver ran through her body: rigours, an unmistakeable sign of infection. She opened her eyes again, squinted at me as if from a great distance, and whispered, 'I am Tina,' and then, 'That's me,' as if to remind herself of her own name.

I took Tina's arm and guided her into my little room, where she gazed uncomprehendingly from the examination bed to the desk to the breastfeeding posters on the wall. I gestured to the chair, and she eased herself into it, her puffa jacket breathing an audible sigh as it crumpled around her.

'Justyna – Tina – I understand you're here for your routine appointment and a review of your ultrasound scan, but you don't look very well. How are you feeling?'

She turned her head towards me – a slow, grinding swivel – and winced. 'I have not been well since four days,' she said. 'It is just cold, I think, or little flu.' Her voice was thin, halting and delicately accented – Polish, I guessed. Recently, a number of Polish shops or *skleps* had opened around the city to cater for a growing immigrant population; Tina's listless demeanour was a stark contrast to the strong, sturdy girls I often saw stacking crates of indigo plums and richly braided breads outside my local *sklep*.

'I have headache and cough,' she continued. 'And very tired. And my ...' She raised a wilting hand towards her collarbone, the dog lead still swinging listlessly around her neck.

'Your throat?' I suggested.

'No, my chest. My chest is hurting. But Monday morning is very busy time for me – I walk dogs, you see, for people when they work – and I am out in the park very early this morning, very cold. I am rushing here for scan and clinic. I need only sleep now. Is just little flu.' She smiled feebly, and I raised a false, fleeting smile in return while I pulled the blood-pressure cuff and thermometer closer to me on the desk.

'Tina, can you slip your arm out of your jacket, please, so I can check your blood pressure?'

She obliged with no small amount of effort, heaving her arm out and pushing the sleeve of her sweatshirt up to reveal waxen-white skin. As I lifted her hand to pass it through the blood-pressure cuff, I realised with a chill that her fingers were icy cold; even her nailbeds were tinted wintry blue. The rigours, the poor circulation, the hollow stare: *If this is 'little flu',* I thought, *then I would hate to see what 'big flu' looks like*. The automated cuff buzzed into life and the machine echoed my thoughts with its own insistent alarm: blood pressure 90/48, pulse 51. I slid the thermometer under Tina's dry, frothy tongue and watched the rise and fall of her chest, counting her respirations at a worryingly high rate of 33 per minute until the thermometer bleeped with its result: 38.7 degrees Celsius.

It is said that moribund patients experience a sense of impending doom, in addition to all of the more obvious, painful symptoms of whatever disease has brought them to death's door. What is less widely known is that midwives also experience this same sensation when their patients begin to deteriorate. Midwife and patient are bound by circumstance, like the hapless stars of an old movie, tied together to a railroad track while a locomotive roars blindly towards their star-crossed embrace. As I scribbled Tina's numbers on the chart in front of me – each one of them flagging a 'red' for urgent action – that fatalistic feeling became very real to me for the first time in my career; I could almost hear the rumble of that oncoming train.

12.58, I wrote. *Preparing to transfer patient to Triage.*

'Tina,' I said, with what I hoped sounded like unwavering confidence, 'I think you may well have the flu, and I think you're very sick. You're my last patient in the clinic, so I'd like to take you back round with me to Triage where we can give you whatever urgent treatment you need.'

'Now?' Her eyes rolled towards mine as she considered my suggestion – my voice seemingly coming to her through a pool of cognitive treacle – and I could almost hear her tired brain wading through this turbid sludge as she tried to process the situation.

'Now,' I replied, and with my hand clutching her arm in an adrenaline-fuelled grip, I guided Tina to standing and steered her out the door. We moved together through the waiting room, along the corridor, past the hospital canteen with its sickeningly dense scent of synthetic beef gravy and, finally, into the din of Triage. On we trudged like some ghoulish four-legged creature, trailing Tina's puffa jacket, case notes and dog lead behind us, oblivious to the stares of the midwives and patients we passed on our way. Tina tripped and sloped along beside me, but I was on a mission, winding a path through the lunchtime crowds until we had reached the relative safety of one of the eight curtained bays in the main Triage treatment room. I helped her onto the bed, where she lay with eerie silence as I slid off her coat and her boots. It was as if, on reaching Triage, she had finally surrendered with mute, easy relief to the illness that had been draining her for days.

While Tina closed her eyes, mine widened with fear. I hustled around the bed, switching on the monitors and punching buttons on the machines, setting them to repeat their observations every few minutes. Blood pressure 86/45. Oxygen 92 per cent. Pulse weak and thready at 49 beats per minute: the slow march of a desperate heart. Worse and worse.

'Excuse me a moment,' I said to Tina, and then I pulled the curtain back and called to Martha, one of the midwives I'd seen at the desk as I'd dragged Tina through the department. 'Page the SHO,' I said, referring to our Senior House Officer, the junior doctor usually responsible for doing initial assessment and basic treatment, and then, looking at Tina's ghostly pallor, I added, 'and the registrar. Sepsis.' A patient as unwell as Tina would need senior review, with a decisive plan and prompt treatment. Martha nodded, set down the notes she'd been reading, and lifted the phone. No further explanation was needed. She and I had battled through dozens of shifts together, and such was our mutual respect and appreciation that we'd developed an easy professional shorthand. A word from me, a nod from Martha; like so many of the bold, ballsy women I worked alongside, I knew she had my back.

As I returned to Tina and watched my machines bleep and beep with progressively worrying numbers, I could feel my own pulse skipping nervously skywards. I was only a few years qualified and it was as if a patient was ticking every box I had been warned about in training; it was almost too horribly perfect to be true. Infection? Tick. High temperature? Tick. Slow pulse, low blood pressure, and cold extremities, as the exhausted heart struggles to pump in the face of an immune system in overdrive? Tick, tick and tick. I knew with an aching certainty that the last box on this morbid checklist was the one marked 'death'. In fact, during my training, death was such a ubiquitous consequence of pretty much every obstetric emergency in the textbook that it became a running joke among the student midwives. Uterus turned inside out as a result of some particularly vigorous cord-pulling? Result: shock, bleeding and death. Allergic reaction to the wrong type of donor blood? Result: shock, organ failure and death. Black coffee with one sugar given to the ward sister instead of the requested tea with milk and two? Result: deep embarrassment, public humiliation, ejection from the hospital aaaaand death, we used to giggle, the prospect of Sister's disapproval seeming much more real to us at that time than the threat of an actual moribund patient. Although I had dealt with some very unwell women by the time I met Tina, none of them had been this far gone. With fresh horror, I realised that I might actually be watching my patient die. *Please not today*, I prayed silently to the Midwifery Gods. *Not on my shift.*

Martha popped her head back round the curtain. 'Both registrars are busy,' she said, as Tina coughed and curled into a tight ball on the bed. 'Labour ward's running two theatres; there's a crash section with twins at thirty-one weeks, and a trial of forceps, with two third-degree tear repairs waiting in the wings, so don't hold your breath.' She looked over at Tina and seemed to register her shocking condition for the first time. 'Fuck,' Martha whispered to me with character-istic bluntness; her assessment of the situation was no less accurate for its brevity. 'I'll see if I can find the SHO.'

I hovered over Tina's bedside, flitting from one monitor to the next, frantically switching off an alarm only for another to start bleeping, until finally the SHO appeared. By this time, Tina's numbers had become even worse: the ones that should have been high were dropping dangerously low, and the ones that should have been low were making an inexorable climb to disaster. Even more worryingly, Tina's attitude had changed from one of dazed exhaustion to acute agitation. Now I wasn't the only one with that textbook sense of impending doom: Tina began to writhe on the bed, her eyes suddenly wild but unseeing.

'What's happening?' she demanded. 'Am I dying? Why do I feel like this?'

I turned to the SHO, who was witnessing this scene with undisguised terror. Raymond was a trainee GP who had not long started his obs and gynae rotation in our hospital; with his gangly physique and a baby-face dusted with the sparse beginnings of a beard, he was often mistaken for a medical student by both patients and staff.

'Where the hell have you been?' I hissed.

Raymond clutched nervously at his ID badge. The photo on it was of an even younger, and much happier, Raymond, grinning broadly on what had probably been the first day of his NHS induction.

'I was in the tea room, updating my Tinder profile,' he whispered as Tina began to clutch wildly at her hair. 'Martha said my picture made me look like a sex pest.'

'For God's sake, Raymond, you could have at least made something up.' I felt a pang of sympathy as Raymond looked duly chastised, but not nearly enough to override my concern for our critically ill patient. 'Tina's a prim at twenty-nine weeks, septic, query flu. She's hypotensive, bradycardic and now ... delirious.'

By this time, Tina was back in the fetal position, arms wrapped around her head, eyes tight shut. Another coughing fit shook her body; even the metal bedframe clattered against the wall with the force of the spasm. 'I can't – I can't catch my breath,' she gasped, her chest heaving. *36 resps per minute*, I guessed, counting silently to myself as she began to chant in a low, urgent voice, 'Make it stop, make it stop, make it stop.'

'I'll need two cannulas, full set of sepsis bloods including culture bottles, a stat bag of fluids, IV paracetamol, a Foleys catheter with urometer, and facial oxygen,' Raymond said.

'You don't say,' I replied, as I showed him the equipment I had already assembled on the bedside trolley. We are well drilled in the assessment and treatment of sepsis; I had done what I could, and needed Raymond to do the rest.

'And amoxicillin.'

'Seriously, Raymond?' I asked, aghast. 'I don't know what they taught you in medical school, but flu is viral. Antibiotics are going to be a waste of time.'

'Just the amoxicillin, please,' he repeated calmly. 'In case this is pneumonia. I'll get on with things here if you and Martha can organise the IVs,' he said, as he unwrapped the various packets required to cannulate Tina and begin the battery of blood tests.

'But it's sepsis secondary to flu,' I said weakly, standing at the end of the bed, now looking at Tina with fresh eyes. 'Or at least … I'm pretty sure it's flu.' Yes, it was flu season; and yes, Tina had initially presented with all of the symptoms we would have expected with flu – she had even, very helpfully, diagnosed herself – but in my rush to do my basic observations and summon the necessary help, I had missed the fact that the clinical picture was rapidly changing. The rapid breathing, low blood pressure, cold hands, burning fever and delirium: I had missed the pneumonial wood for the proverbial trees.

Within the next twenty minutes, we had stabilised Tina and initiated the appropriate treatment. Martha had gathered the IV paracetamol, fluids and antibiotics, and started running them through the cannulas Raymond had sited in both hands. With the situation now under control, I had finally managed to listen in to Tina's baby (whose heartbeat was remarkably steady and clear, under the circumstances) and Raymond had updated both registrars, and was now on the phone to one of the senior medics in the general hospital adjoining our building. Tina was to stay with us until a porter became available to transfer her to the main receiving unit, where her care would continue under specialist guidance. Everyone had played their part, the team had pulled together, and although Tina was by no means out of danger, things were moving in the right direction.

While Raymond was making his phone calls and almost a dozen little multicoloured vials of Tina's blood were winging their way to various branches of the hospital laboratories, I sat at the foot of Tina's bed. Triage had emptied out, as it sometimes does in the lull between the lunchtime rush and the late-afternoon deluge, and beyond our little curtained bay, the department was quiet save for the distant ringing of a telephone and the gentle smack of Martha's trainers across the floor. As another bag of IV fluids dripped steadily into her veins, Tina had once again settled into stillness, eyes closed, body soft and slack on the bed.

'Tina …?' I ventured. 'Are you still here?'

'Mmm.'

I searched my brain for a topic that would engage her, that would keep her in the room. And then I saw the old yellow dog lead hanging limply over the head of the bed.

'Do you have any dogs of your own, Tina?'

She nodded, then grimaced and raised an icy, white hand to her neck.

'What are their names?'

Tina opened her eyes, looked at me, thought hard. 'I have Poodle called Marco, and spaniel called Bibi. And also I have … black, no, brown dog, called …' She closed her eyes again, pressed them tight in concentration, then looked back at me apologetically. 'I'm sorry. I can't remember.'

It was alarming to see that even though Tina's body had been coaxed back from the brink of collapse, the haze of disease still clouded her mind. For a 'dog person', to forget the name and colour of your pet is akin to forgetting the identities of your children – a sure sign of cognitive compromise. I scrambled in my pocket for my phone, pressed a button and the lock screen flashed up: a photo of my Boston Terrier wearing a daft pink tartan tie after a visit to the groomer. It crossed my mind that this level of sharing was highly unprofessional, and I began to play out a Single White Female scenario in my mind, wherein Tina embarked on a relentless stalking campaign, lurking outside my house every evening in a pink tartan necktie – but as she squinted and focused her eyes on the image, Tina smiled broadly, brilliantly.

'Ahh, your dog is lovely,' she said, and for the first time since she'd set foot in that small, windowless room in the clinic, I felt as though I was actually meeting the real Tina. Amidst the drips, wires, machines and monitors, for a brief moment we were two sentimental dog owners, cooing over my 'fur baby'.

The door opened. It was Raymond, stethoscope flung round his neck, cheeks flushed, scrub trousers dragging low enough to reveal the top of his pink-and-blue-striped boxer shorts. I wondered if his mother still bought his underwear. He grinned and beckoned for me to come outside. I squeezed Tina's hand, pulled the curtain closed behind me and followed Raymond out to the desk.

'They've got a bed for Tina over the way …'

'That's great, Raymond.' I was truly, genuinely, physically relieved to hear that soon Tina would be the responsibility of a team whose staff were more accustomed to dealing with critically ill patients.

'And guess what? I got three matches on Tinder while I was cannulating your patient. Fucking yassss!' He raised his hand to high-five me. Well, it would have been rude to leave him hanging, and he did just help to save my patient's life. I high-fived him, low-fived him, and we may have even shared a little fist-bump before he shuffled back to the desk.

One of the most difficult things about Triage is that we seldom get to see the end of our patients' stories. As the name of the unit suggests, they come in for assessment, get triaged to the appropriate department, have a baby or get sent home. Whatever happens, happens, while our phone keeps ringing and the waiting room keeps filling up. Over the next few weeks, I would use any spare moment to search for Tina's lab results on our online system, curious about her outcome, wondering if she would ever remember the names of all her dogs, or even see them again, or stride through the woods with a flush in her cheeks as the pack yomped happily through the trees ahead. As days passed and the lab results rolled in one by one, the diagnosis was confirmed: influenza, complicated by pneumonia. A double dunter, as they say. So Raymond and I had both been right.

Some time later, as Triage began to bloom with early springtime babies, Tina returned to our desk. She looked radiant, powerful and strong as she breathed through wave after wave of contractions. I would barely have recognised her if I hadn't seen her name on the front of her notes. As it was, she didn't recognise me at all.

I took Tina's arm and guided her gently towards bed five, a few steps from where she'd been during that terrifying time in December, and I smiled to myself as she made the unmistakeable sounds of a woman in the advanced stages of labour. A torrent of Polish expletives spilled from her mouth as a mighty surge rolled through her body; she was brimming with life in all of its brutal glory despite the spectre of death that had lingered at her back. As she raged and roared, I said a silent prayer in praise of whatever merciful force had kept Tina safe. I thanked the Oracle, I thanked Martha, and I even thanked Raymond.

Notes on Being from Somewhere Else

My father has this bag.

He keeps it in a safety deposit box in the bank in my home town; a squat, red-brick building that sits between a pharmacy and a hair salon. There are other things in the box – a life's worth of papers and trinkets – but the bag has an almost magical quality in spite of its homespun appearance. I suppose you could call it a primitive travel pouch, an early ancestor of the Velcro-pocketed bum bags sold on revolving display stands at airports and train stations. But my father's bag has no Velcro and no clever pockets; it's just a little sack, hand-sewn from two squares of burlap, now worn smooth from years of use, with a long, skinny strap. Big enough to hold a passport, a folded sheaf of bills, and perhaps a photograph or two, but small enough to be concealed under clothing, hidden from fellow travellers who share your route, but not your intentions.

The bag belonged to my father's father, who wore it close to his body when he fled Ukraine in the early twentieth century. It wasn't very popular to be Jewish in that time and place; your house was liable to be set alight in the night, your brothers and sisters cowering under the kitchen table. So my grandfather left when he was still young enough to make a new life somewhere else, and he took the bag, and he crossed a strange sea to Canada.

My mother doesn't even have a bag. Her father, a young Czech lawyer with a promising career ahead of him, was warned by a neighbour one day that he was likely to be killed by invading Nazis the next. He disappeared by dawn, walking first out of the city he loved, then into the forest, then across the border into Poland, where friends awaited who could speed his safe passage to England. My mother's mother was luckier in that her exodus from the same country began not on foot, but on a train. At just fourteen years old, she was waved off at the station by her parents, whose grim smiles belied the bone-deep knowledge that they would never see her again. No cases or bags remain from those desperate journeys – only the stories passed down in the safety deposit box of our family history.

So I'm 100 per cent refugee, although you would never know it. My skin is the right colour to pass as 'White British', although I often find myself ticking the 'White Other' box on questionnaires and applications. My voice has a socially acceptable accent, only the odd twang betraying traces of my most recent migration, from America to Britain, nearly twenty years ago. I fly under the radar, and when others comment on incomers with their odd ways and unappealing needs, I know that my blood is the same blood of those grandparents whose survival depended on the kindness of strangers – strangers who accepted their ways, and met their needs.

This history has not only given me an acute sense of gratitude to those faceless strangers, but a strange sense of kinship with the women who have fled war and persecution to end up in my care. I've met waves of immigrants from the world's notorious hotspots of death and destruction, and when I read the stories and see the scars of these women, I'm compelled – perhaps naively – to acknowledge their stories, to soothe their scars, and maybe, in some small way, to repay the kindness that enabled my grandparents to survive and to thrive. In another life, it could have been me waving goodbye to my parents through a smoke-blackened window or cowering behind a tree as the boots of enemy soldiers snapped pine branches strewn on a dark forest floor. I look at my children, who have been raised in peace and comfort, and marvel that anyone could want them dead simply because of some tenuous link to race or religion; and yet, unless the forces of good in this world continue to triumph over the dark tides of hatred and bigotry, it could still be so.

Of course, not every immigrant with a tale of woe has a heart of gold, and I don't always get it right. I've spent honey-tongued hours at the bedside of a sorry-looking soul from far away, cooing over her pain, bringing her trays of sweet tea and biscuits, only to be told by another patient that the woman's 'sister' was busy rifling through the filing cabinets in our office, filling her pockets with whatever goodies the NHS could provide. On another recent shift in the postnatal ward, I took a handover about a patient whose journey from a well-known war zone almost had me in tears. I fetched a jug of fresh water and approached the bed space with my most beatific smile.

'Welcome, and congratulations,' I purred, enunci-ating each word slowly and clearly in case she was still struggling with this new language. 'Can I help you?' She pointed to the brand-new mobile phone by her side, with its rose-gold, diamanté case, then to the woman cuddling a newborn in the opposite bed, and said in clear, virtually unaccented English, 'This woman – she has iPhone charger?'

Sometimes, though, I meet a woman who truly has nothing: not a phone, or a word of English, or even a biscuit in her grumbling, grasping stomach. She doesn't know it, but we have something in common. And I can help.

Pei Hsuan:
I Have Carried This Story

There was someone in the waiting room who didn't belong there.

It was a busy Monday morning in Triage, and the fire alarm had gone off just as a dozen patients had filed in to the department. Women of all colours, shapes and sizes lifted their heads and searched frantically for the source of the shrieking sound, like a startled flock of exotic birds, their magazines flapping to the floor. I peered at the fire system control panel with Betty and Madge, the other midwives for the day.

'Ground-floor toilets,' Betty mused, pointing to one of the flashing lights on the panel. 'Some poor sod's been rumbled having a fag. Never mind, I could do with one myself. Grab your coats, girls,' she said, and headed for the door.

Madge and I pulled on our standard-issue navy fleeces and made a mental tally of the women in the department: this one with the black puffa coat and the three screaming toddlers; that one with the niqab and the Louis Vuitton handbag; the two identical twins, both pregnant, who were buttoning their bellies into identical red duffel coats.

'Everybody out,' called Madge, corralling the crowd through the double doors and into the corridor. 'Let's go and look at the pretty firemen,' she added, winking back at me over her shoulder.

Fire alarms being an increasingly common occurrence within the hospital, Madge and I were more than familiar with this ritual. Midwives and auxiliaries were forever burning snacks in contraband toasters and forbidden George Foreman grills – such costly and disruptive accidents were the reason why only a select few departments had been granted the lesser-spotted, and much longed-for 'Toaster Authorisation Form'. We marched into the frosty January morning along with dozens of other women who'd been hurried out of clinics and scans; the fire alarm screamed into the crisp blue sky as staff and patients mingled and chattered, waiting in giggly anticipation for the fire engine that arrived not long after. The engine's doors opened and released a crew of firefighters who were in no particular hurry to run the gauntlet of a hundred hormonal females; there were the usual jokes about long hoses and fireman's lifts as the men trudged past us to investigate. Ten minutes passed and by the time the firemen lumbered back out, grumbling about 'another bloody waste of time', the assembled crowd had begun to feel the chill: coats were drawn tight and scarves double-wrapped as we shuffled against each other to keep warm. The hospital boss appeared with a clipboard and started waving women back into the building as the fire truck rumbled away.

'Who the hell is that?' said Betty, as she ground out her furtively smoked cigarette under the toe of her battered black trainers.

'Big Boss,' replied Madge. 'I've only ever seen her twice – once during another fire alarm, and once when they tried to sack me for too many sickies. Obviously,' she said, grinning, 'I'm still here.'

We plunged our hands into our fleece pockets and joined the herd of women moving back into the building. The door to the toilets next to the reception desk hung open, but there was no sign of a fire.

'What was it?' I asked Patience, one of the ward sisters who was ushering onlookers past the toilet door.

'Someone was smoking crack; the firemen found the gear in the lavvy pan,' she stage-whispered as she rolled her eyes. 'Classy clientele.'

Once Betty, Madge and I had made it back to the desk, we surveyed the women who had resumed their positions in the waiting room, many of whom were now looking pointedly at their watches and huffing to each other about the delay and the cold.

'Kayden, stop poking your sister's eye!' shouted the woman in the puffa to one of her toddlers, with little effect. The woman in the niqab clutched her Louis Vuitton closer to her chest, while the twins busied themselves taking selfies on matching iPhones. All present and correct, plus one.

While most of the women in the waiting room were still peeling off woolly layers as they settled back into their stiff plastic chairs, a young Chinese woman wearing only a faded green T-shirt, grey sweatpants and flip-flops hovered next to the vending machines by the door. She seemed unsure whether to cross the threshold into the department, and her eyes darted back and forth as she ran her hands nervously across her belly, which was just round enough to hold either an average-sized five-month fetus, or a severely stunted baby at full term. Her frame was slight and girlish, but there was a steeliness to her gaze and a grim set to her jaw, which made her age impossible to determine.

'Who's that?' I asked Betty.

She looked up, then back down at the pile of case notes for the women who had phoned the department that morning and been invited in for assessment: Watson, McNee, Hirschberg, Al-Hamza, Khan, Khan and Willoughby. 'Not here,' she said. 'No idea. But she looks right up your street.' I had already developed a reputation within Triage for gravitating towards the vulnerable, the lost and, sometimes, the ever so slightly crazy. Betty knew my style, and was happy enough to leave these patients to me. 'I'm with Watson,' she said, and she called the first patient into the treatment area.

I walked over to the girlish figure by the door. She quaked slightly as I approached, as if she were fighting some inner impulse to run, but a competing, stronger urge compelled her to hold her ground. Even standing at what I hoped was a non-threatening distance, I could smell her: the sour, salty tang of the unwashed, and the ketotic, pear-drop breath of the hungry. On closer inspection, there were seams of dirt in the creases of her fingers, and the hem of her top was soiled and frayed.

'Can I help you?' I asked.

She squinted at me with intense concentration, searching my face for signs of trustworthiness or malice. After a long moment of scrutiny, she must have decided that she was satisfied with what she saw. Her body eased, her shoulders dropping fractionally, her jaw a bit less tense. She reached into the pocket of her sweatpants, withdrew a square of tightly folded paper, and extended her hand to me as if passing a baton.

I took the paper. It was as smooth as suede, the surface lightly furred from being fingered, clutched, grasped and stroked, the edges beginning to split from being folded and re-folded countless times. As I lifted a corner of the paper and began to open it out as carefully as I could, the woman stared with a stern, hawkish focus, like an archivist watching a bumbling researcher fumble with her most precious ancient text. The moment seemed to call for white cotton gloves and the hush of an oak-panelled library, not the clamour and cloying heat of the Triage waiting room.

As I gingerly unfolded the sheet, I could see that it was a piece of lined A4, the same kind my daughters used for their homework, but instead of sums or spelling tests, this paper was crammed from top to bottom with what I guessed were Mandarin characters. Some of it was written in pen, some in barely visible pencil, some in large characters, some small, as if the author had added to the page at different times, in different moods, with whatever implement had been available. As I squinted at the page, I could decipher neatly printed numbers here and there among the scrawl – 2017, 2018 – and I wondered whether this paper represented some kind of chronology. Whatever it was, it was clearly precious to its bearer. I passed it back to her, and she carefully re-folded it until it was small enough to hide within her tightly clenched fist.

The woman spoke, then, in a language I didn't understand – *ni hao*, or hello, was as far as my Mandarin went – and pointed to herself, then back at the sheet of A4. Her voice was as soft and ragged as the paper I had held in my hand, but there was an unmistakeable urgency to what she was saying.

As the waiting room continued to fill, and the phones rang noisily at the desk, I knew that this woman would need my undivided attention for the next hour;

possibly for the rest of the morning. I could see Betty and Madge shuttling busily from the treatment room to the desk, ferrying urine samples, swabs and sheaves of paperwork back and forth. Soraya, the doctor, appeared at the desk, but disappeared again just as quickly when her pager went off with its urgent beeping. Triage was 'going like a fair', as we often said, and at times like these, all hands were required to keep the department running smoothly. However, there was also the tacit agreement among staff that, sometimes, one urgent patient took precedence over three others with less pressing concerns. This hierarchy of need was the true meaning of triage, and while the woman in front of me might not have been haemorrhaging, rigouring with fever or pushing out a baby, everything about her cried out for help, including – I felt – the indecipherable scrawl I had held in my hand.

'Come with me,' I said, and I nodded towards one of the department's single side rooms, where the woman could have the still, peaceful sanctuary she clearly needed. As we walked to the room, Madge passed in the other direction, a cardboard pot of urine in her hand.

'I'm going to be off the floor for a little while,' I said. 'Sorry.'

'Whatever,' she drawled as she strode on towards the sluice, the little pot sloshing precariously as she walked. 'Do what you gotta do.'

As Madge disappeared down the corridor, I ushered my new patient into the room and closed the door gently behind us. She flinched as it clicked shut, and I smiled to try and put her at ease.

'You can wait here,' I said, and I patted the starched white sheets on the bed. 'It's OK. I have to organise a few things for you now, but I will be back. I promise.'

She looked at me questioningly, uncomprehendingly. How could I let her know that I would return and that I would try to help her? Suddenly, I remembered that my mobile phone was in the side pocket of my navy-blue cargo trousers. I fished it out and tapped on the app I used sometimes when a labourer pitched up at the desk, crying out in a foreign language with no official translator to hand.

English to Mandarin, I typed, and then, *Are you in pain?*

I held out my phone to the woman. She peered at the screen, seemed to recognise the familiar characters of the translation, and shook her head. She looked back at me expectantly; there was something she was waiting for me to ask.

Are you bleeding? I typed.

Again, a shake of the head.

I was satisfied that this wasn't a medical emergency, but still, the woman had locked her eyes onto mine in expectation. I turned back to the phone and typed, *Are you hungry?*

A wave of recognition, and then relief, passed over her face. She nodded.

I will bring food, I typed, and again, I could see her relax. *And I will get an interpreter.* She nodded again, quicker this time, and pointed to the phone, waving her finger towards the screen for emphasis. She had something to tell me; that much was clear.

I turned towards the door, then stopped and turned back. I tapped again on my phone, and extended it to the woman one last time. *You will be safe here.* The worried twist of her mouth softened into a wide smile, and she sat back onto the clean sheets behind her.

I began to compile a mental to-do list as I walked to the desk. Tess, one of the unit's auxiliaries, was peering at her clipboard, wondering why the waiting room was full of twice as many women as there were names on her list.

'Tess, could you bring a tray of tea, biscuits and whatever sandwiches we've got to the lady in the side room?'

She arched an eyebrow. 'Feeding a football team, are we?'

'No,' I said, 'she's just – she's just really hungry.'

'Vegetarian? Halal? Coeliac?' droned Tess, going through our patients' most commonly expressed dietary restrictions. 'Because I think all we've got is corned beef. If it's even in date.'

My own stomach rumbled as if in sympathy with the woman who was waiting to be fed a few metres away. The fire alarm meant that we had all missed our breakfast break, and the way the day was going, we probably wouldn't see lunch until at least late after-noon, when every patient had been assessed and dispatched to the appropriate corner of the hospital. I wondered if my patient was still sitting on the bed, or pacing the floor. Perhaps she had even left already while my back was turned, slipping out the door and away from the department as silently as she'd crept in. I pictured her shivering outside under the cold

January sun; sitting at a bus shelter, unnoticed by commuters huffing and tutting about the delayed service; walking down a dark street, the last of the dry winter leaves crunching beneath her flip-flops.

'Whatever we've got, Tess,' I said. 'And lots of it.'

Next on the list: I needed to contact the interpreting service, to unlock the secrets of this woman's folded paper and give her the help she needed, but the phone wouldn't stop ringing long enough for me to make an outgoing call.

'Triage, Midwife Hazard, how can I help you?' I said quickly.

'What it is, is, I'm going to Tenerife next Sunday and I wanted to ask if a spray tan would hurt my baby, because I've googled it and ...'

'Please call back.' The phone rang again the second the handset hit the receiver.

'Triage. Hello.'

'So, my hairdresser saw this thing online about pre-eclampsia, and my left pinky toe looks a bit swollen this morning, so ...'

'Please call back!' Again, I slammed the phone down, immediately lifting it back up to dial the number before it had a chance to ring again.

'Interpreting Services, do you need telephone or face-to-face?'

'Face-to-face, please.'

'Which language, and for when?'

'Mandarin. As soon as possible, please.'

I could hear fingers rattling across a keyboard on the other end of the line, and snatches of a radio advertisement for holidays in the sun. I drummed my own fingers on the desk. Through the doorway to the treatment room, I could see Madge wafting a green-tinged sanitary pad in front of Betty's face; Betty's nose wrinkled in disgust and she play-punched Madge's shoulder.

'I have Mandarin for you, ma'am. There's an interpreter finishing with another woman in Outpatients – will I ask her to come round?'

'Yes, please,' I sighed with relief.

I ran from the desk before the phone could ring again. In the side room, the woman was sitting cross-legged on the bed. She had kicked her flip-flops onto the floor, and the soles of her feet were black and creased with dirt. Tess had set a red plastic hospital tray in front of her, and in the brief time that I had been at the desk, the woman must have eaten everything she had been given. Two empty sandwich packets sat on the tray, along with four empty biscuit wrappers, an empty Lucozade bottle, and a squat hospital teacup that held only the thinnest dregs of murky liquid. The woman looked slightly dazed after this feast; she leaned back against the stiff white pillows and closed her eyes while her fingers drew lazy circles over the arc of her belly.

I was clearing the tray to a trolley against the wall when the door opened behind me. The woman gave a start and regarded the intruder with sidelong suspicion. It was May, an elegant Chinese lady, her hair neatly lacquered into a smooth bob, her burgundy velvet blazer carefully coordinated with her bag and shoes. I had met May before, with other patients: she was efficient, articulate and discreet, and I was glad of her presence. She nodded to me and introduced herself to the woman in Mandarin; the woman responded in a rush of words, her tone urgent, her hands gesticulating wildly. She withdrew the folded paper from the pocket of her sweatpants, and began to open it out again, her voice rising as she did so.

May listened carefully, then turned to me. 'She says she has a story to tell you. She wants you to sit, and to listen.'

Maybe I should tell her to wait, I thought. Maybe I should examine her first – listen to her baby, check her blood pressure – before she launches into a story that could tie me up for the rest of the day. I could hear the muffled sounds of footsteps and conversation beyond the closed door, and I knew all too well how busy Madge and Betty would be with the other patients, but something about the insistence in this woman's voice made my own words catch in my throat. May drew up a chair and sat beside the bed, and I followed in silent obedience. The woman smoothed her paper out on the bed in front of her, as if preparing to read from a holy scroll. She took a long, deep breath, rolled her shoulders back, and began to speak. As she did so, May cocked her head to the side, listening intently, then relayed the words to me in English as the tale unfolded:

"'My name is Pei Hsuan Liu,'" May began. "'I have carried this story for a very long time, in very ...'" Here, the woman's voice cracked, and May hesitated before continuing. "'In very difficult circumstances.'" Pei Hsuan looked down at her paper and drew breath again. "'I am from Fujian province. My mother and father had a duck farm; it was small, but the ducks were the finest for many miles around, and we did well. Even when my sister was born, my parents still bought me warm clothes and good books for school. I was clever; I wanted to be a teacher. But our luck was bad, and two years ago, on the twelfth of December, my mother died suddenly. My father took it very hard. He drank. He stopped working. He stayed in bed. My sister and I tried to tend the farm and do our school work, but it was too much. We struggled through the winter until the eighteenth of March last year, when a man we did not know was waiting for us outside our school. He said our father had paid him many yuan to send us to the UK, where we could have a better life, and become wealthy.'"

Here, Pei Hsuan let out a sharp, bitter laugh. May paused, and then took up the story as Pei Hsuan continued:

"'We did not believe that even our father, who was sad and sick, would have made this plan to send us away, and we fought, but the man was strong. He took us in his car and we drove for many hours, until it was dark and we reached a house we had never seen before. There were other girls there, and in the morning, we were all given fake passports and told that we would be flying to London. I cried, but the man beat me, and when he said he would beat my sister too, I stopped. Six of us were driven to the airport and put on a flight. We were terrified of the aeroplane, and we had been told not to speak until we landed. It was ..."' Pei Hsuan paused, and May paused, until a shadow passed over Pei Hsuan's face and she resumed. "'It was a difficult journey.'"

"'In London,'" she continued, "'we were again taken to a house where there were many girls, some from China, even from Fujian, some from Nigeria, Vietnam, Iraq. We worked for a woman called Fan, and we worked ...'" Again, that shadow across her face like a cloud. "'We worked very hard, with many men. I did not believe that men could do such things, and I cried every night for what my sister and I had to do, but Fan would beat us every time we complained, and tell us that our father had sent us away because we were worthless. Eventually, I had no more tears, but my sister cried and fought every night. It was hard for her. She was only a child.'" May's voice broke and she became silent while Pei Hsuan rattled on in Mandarin. May listened, head still to the side, eyes widening, until she seemed to remember her role as interpreter, and she picked up the story again in English.

"'I am seventeen, but my sister was only thirteen,'" May whispered. We looked at each other. Pei Hsuan carried on, and May resumed.

"'My sister fought every night, and every night she was beaten, and every time, the beatings got worse, and Fan said that she would kill her if she did not behave. On the sixth of June, it was very hot, and I worked very hard. By the morning, I had been with eight men, and when I finished, my sister was gone. I have not seen her since then. I begged Fan to tell me where she was taken, and I promised to work so hard that I would pay for her to come back. Fan made me work twice as hard, but my sister never returned, and by September, I realised that my belly was growing. By December, the men stopped wanting me, and Fan told me she would get rid of me like she had got rid of my sister. On the seventh of January, I was taken from my bed and put in a van, again with other girls. There were no windows, and we were very cold, and after many hours, some of the girls began to say that we would die. At last we stopped. It was in your city. The driver opened the doors and asked which one of us was the one with the baby. He threw me out of the van, and drove away. And I have walked. I have walked and walked, and I have found you.'"

May folded her hands in her lap and waited for me to reply, but I was speechless. Of course, I knew about human trafficking. It wasn't uncommon for us to have our suspicions about how women in our care had been treated, or to look after patients who were putting their lives together with the help of numerous agencies after surviving an ordeal similar to the one Pei Hsuan had described. But this was the first time that a woman had been thrown out of the back of a van and had landed in my lap, so to speak. For Pei Hsuan, I was the first point of contact. I was it.

'Pei Hsuan,' I began. She looked at me expectantly. Her features seemed softer now that she had unburdened herself, and although the sandwiches and biscuits hadn't filled the hollows in her cheeks, I could see her now for the scared seventeen-year-old she really was. I decided to begin with the basics. 'What you've been through is horrible, but you're in a place now where people will help you. I can begin to do that, but first, would you like me to listen to your baby?'

Her jaw tightened again, and she spoke in Mandarin. "'I don't want this baby,'" May translated. "'This baby has many fathers, and all of them are evil.'"

May and I exchanged glances. It would be hard enough to find Pei Hsuan the emergency help she needed, but even harder to address the medical and moral complexities of sustaining a pregnancy that was unwanted, yet too far progressed to terminate.

'It will take me a little while to organise the help that you need today,' I began, as May relayed my words. 'I need to make some phone calls, but while I do that, the doctor will do a quick scan, and talk things over. May will stay with you so you can tell us all what you need.' I moved towards the door, then turned back to the miserable figure sitting cross-legged on the bed. 'I promise you, as long as you're in this building, you're safe.' I waited to make sure that May had translated this last message, and then I let the door close softly behind me.

Stepping back into the waiting room was like being teleported onto the floor of a stock exchange in the middle of a trading frenzy. The department was still full, but in the time that I had been sitting with Pei Hsuan, the old faces had been replaced with new ones, no less irate or impatient than the last. Couples were arguing above the clatter of the phones and gesticulating angrily towards the treatment area, where every bed was occupied. Soraya was having a heated debate with Madge at the desk, and I braced myself for the crossfire.

'Soraya,' I began. She and Madge both glared at me as the phones rang incessantly behind them. 'I have a seventeen-year-old prim of unknown gestation who's been trafficked into this country and had no antenatal care.' Soraya raised one perfectly threaded eyebrow. 'Could you scan her quickly while I make a few calls? She has nowhere to live, no money, nothing.'

'What are we today, the Red Cross?' Madge snapped. 'Seriously, Hazard, one patient all morning? It's like the Battle of the fecking Somme out here.'

'I'm sorry.' She had a fair point. There was work to be done – a department full of women in pain and distress – and Pei Hsuan had been tying me up. At the same time, I knew I couldn't do a cursory examination and toss her back out the door. Not for the first time, I thought of my own relatives who had arrived on foreign shores with little more than the clothes on their backs, and of the nameless strangers who must have helped them. For Pei Hsuan, I was one of those strangers, and I had made a promise. 'I'll make these calls, and then I can start seeing somebody else.'

'Halle-bloody-lujah,' Madge replied, and she lumbered off to the treatment area while Soraya headed for Pei Hsuan in the side room. The desk was mine, if only the phones would stop ringing.

Contrary to the opinion held by some of my colleagues, I am not actually a one-woman refugee camp, and my knowledge of resources for women with absolutely nothing was, well, similarly scant. It was now early afternoon, and it was Friday, and I knew that if I didn't expand my knowledge of the system within the next few hours, Pei Hsuan would remain in homeless, hungry limbo all weekend, or she might even decide to disappear back into the crowd in which she'd arrived.

Within the next hectic hour, I'd made a volley of calls back and forth to every local charity for refugees and asylum seekers, been put through to three different branches of the Home Office, listened to the soothing tones of hold music while the hurricane of Triage swirled around me, and finally managed to speak to someone who could open a case for Pei Hsuan and organise emergency accommodation for her in a hostel across town.

'Thank you so much,' I said to the faceless helper on the other end of the phone. One by one, I was adding to Pei Hsuan's team of supporters; a small but growing counterbalance to the abusers she had known. 'That's amazing. Do you have any idea how we can get transport for this lady? I wish I could put her in a taxi, but the hospital doesn't have funds for this kind of thing.'

'We'll send a driver from ... let me see ...' She hesitated, and then named a private contractor. 'He'll have a job number. Should be with you by four o'clock if you can keep your patient until then.'

My heart dropped. The company she had named was a government subcontractor that had been assigned a number of previously state-run services, from prisons and detention centres to hostels and hospitals, and it had been in the news recently for all manner of alleged mistreatment and neglect of the vulnerable migrants in its care. But even beyond these allegations, there was one word in the Home Office official's reply that filled me with dread: 'he'. Even after listening to Pei Hsuan's story, and promising to help, and even in spite of my subtle sense of kinship with this girl from the other side of the world, it would all come down to one thing: I would be just another stranger passing my human cargo into the hands of an unknown man.

'That's … that's fine,' I said to the woman on the phone. 'I'll keep an eye out for him.'

I replaced the phone in its receiver, only for it to ring again immediately. And again, and again. The afternoon wore on in this way, the department teeming with women, the phone ringing, the staff bobbing and weaving through it all like battle-zone stretcher-bearers dodging the whip and zing of enemy bullets. While Pei Hsuan (and what, Soraya told me, appeared to be a thirty-week fetus) waited in the side room, I did my best to carry on with my normal working day. I saw two bleeding women, a rupture of membranes, a preterm labourer, four reduced movements, and a woman who had fainted in the Outpatients waiting room, which was even more tightly packed than the one in Triage. By the time a sandy-haired man in a blue bomber jacket approached the desk at half past four, I had almost managed to push Pei Hsuan to a corner of my mind, but when he presented me with his corporate ID badge, she sprang back to the forefront with whiplash speed.

'I'm here to pick up a patient,' he said. He took a folded scrap of paper from his pocket – smaller and less worn than Pei Hsuan's – and squinted at it as he attempted to read her name. 'Pay Shoon, it says here. Or something like that.' He flashed a quick smile at me. 'Be a sweetheart and be quick about it, if you don't mind. I've got another three to collect before I clock off, and the traffic's a bloody nightmare.'

I didn't feel like being quick about it, and after the day I'd had, I certainly didn't feel like being a sweet-heart. Not for this man, not for anyone. But what choice did I have? I couldn't head home that night without knowing that I had done my best to find Pei Hsuan her own accommodation, however basic, and I couldn't refuse to hand her over to the driver on the very thin grounds that he was a man. Did he seem trustworthy? I couldn't tell. Did he seem pleasant? It was a moot point. I couldn't even ask him for any further proof of his identity or legitimacy; he had shown me his ID straight away, exactly as protocol dictated.

'Is that your girl's lift, Hazard?' Betty asked as she passed the desk. 'About time. She'll be better off out of this madhouse,' she said, nodding towards the side room. 'She'll be in there, wishing she'd never come.'

I raised a weak smile in reply as the driver shifted impatiently from foot to foot. 'Come with me,' I said.

Pei Hsuan was sleeping, her tiny body curled into a ball, her bare feet overlapping like the wings of a bird. She was alone. May had left at two o'clock, called to another interpreting job in a different part of the hospital. She'd heard many stories, and would hear many more, all different, all urgent, but each one filtered by her from mother tongue to English, the language of the system.

'Pei Hsuan,' I whispered, rousing her as gently as I could. Her eyes snapped open, and her gaze darted from me to the man whose unfamiliar bulk filled the door frame behind me. 'This man will take you to your home for the night.' Inwardly, I cursed myself for speaking loudly and slowly, as if to a child. *Idiot*, I told myself. *She's got no idea what you're saying*. I couldn't even use my phone to translate; the battery had died hours ago. Instead, I smiled awkwardly and gestured to the driver, who winked and raised his hand to his forehead, pretending to doff an invisible cap. Pei Hsuan drew herself slowly up to sitting, and slipped her feet into the flip-flops on the floor, but she seemed glued to the bed by inertia, or terror, or both.

'Please, Pei Hsuan,' I said, trying to mask the desperation in my voice, and hoping that she would at least understand my best intentions. 'He will take you to a safe place. Please.' I guided her towards the door with heavy feet. The corners of my mouth were smiling, but my cheeks were frozen.

'All right, love,' the driver chirped to Pei Hsuan as he turned to leave. And then, over his shoulder, with another wink, 'As they say, chop-chop!'

He marched into the waiting room and strode towards the exit. Pei Hsuan took one last, long look at me, surveying me coolly from top to toe. What did she see? A kindly stranger with goodwill in her heart, or another link in the chain, passing her thoughtlessly into the waiting hands of another man, who would take her to another crowded flat, packed to the rafters with another tragic gaggle of lost and lonely girls? Pei Hsuan's expression was inscrutable. After a moment that seemed to hold a lifetime of disappointment, she turned her head and body as one, and with a slow, shuffling gait, she followed the driver out of the department, her flip-flops scuffing the floor as she went.

Notes on Baby Brain

There was a magical moment somewhere towards the end of my second pregnancy when I found myself in the kitchen late at night, standing in the glow of the open refrigerator, cradling a toaster in my arms. Having made myself a slice of buttery toast, I had unplugged the toaster, carefully coiled its cord around its still-warm body and opened the fridge. I was moments away from placing the toaster on the middle shelf in between a tub of hummus and a half-eaten chocolate cake. I had performed this sequence of movements fluidly, unquestioningly, as if unplugging one's toaster and storing it in the fridge was the most natural and logical thing to do. At the last second, some distant spark of common sense fired in my brain and I realised that perhaps the toaster really ought to remain in its usual nest of crumbs on the worktop. *Ah*, I thought to myself, surveying the contents of the fridge as if I'd suddenly awoken from a sleepwalking episode. *Baby brain.*

I was amused – and maybe even a little bit proud – to find myself suddenly victim to one of the most widely known foibles of modern pregnancy. To suffer from 'baby brain' – whether late at night, in front of the fridge with a toaster in your arms, or in the supermarket, wondering what on earth you came in for – is almost a rite of passage. It's a sign that yes, while your body has shown the outward signs of pregnancy for a while, your mind has finally followed suit in universally accepted, frazzled fashion – like a modern version of 'hysteria', the archaic, catch-all term once used to describe any kind of female behaviour which deviated inconveniently from the norm. In the good old days of shit-and-sawdust asylums and psychological quackery, a diagnosis of hysteria (a word whose Greek translation means, quite literally, 'a condition of the womb') could easily damn a woman to a lifetime of brutal and humiliating abuse disguised as 'treatment'. While hysteria is, thankfully, no longer recognised as a legitimate psychological ailment, could it be that 'baby brain' is its harmless-sounding, more socially acceptable descendant? We may no longer lock women up for being strange or silly, but there still seems to be a need to pathologise – and find quaint, cosy nicknames for – the normal flux of the female psyche.

Even the most progressive contemporary psychologists and neuroscientists have yet to reach a consensus on what actually happens to a woman's brain during pregnancy and early parenthood. Does she get stupid or smart? Does she become more introverted and oblivious to the world around her as she focuses on her baby? Or is she more switched on to the emotional and physical cues of those closest to her, thus giving her an evolutionary advantage as she attempts to bond with, and care for, her offspring? In spite of copious research, no one seems able to say with any certainty what happens inside the weird and wonderful brain of a woman as she makes the transition to motherhood. Like Mel Gibson puzzling over the opposite sex in the now amusingly dated film *What Women Want*, much of modern science seems to look at pregnant women, scratch its head and drag its knuckles onwards down the laboratory corridor.

What is clear, though, is that perinatal mental health is becoming a hot topic and an urgent cause for concern. There is a growing body of international evidence around the subject, with studies of varying focus and intent arriving at the same conclusion: the emotional toll of early motherhood is more pervasive and complex than has previously been thought. Recent evidence from the UK suggests that as many as one in five women experience problems with their mental health during pregnancy and the first year after birth. To put that statistic in context, this means that in some areas, the odds of a woman experiencing poor perinatal mental health are higher than her odds of having a forceps birth, and almost as high as her baby being delivered by Caesarean section – and these are only the women we know about. In addition to those who are sick enough and/or brave enough to seek help with their mental health and to receive a diagnosis of depression, anxiety or even postnatal psychosis, I can say from experience that there must be thousands, even millions of women, around the world who struggle with the massive physical and emotional challenges of pregnancy and parenthood without admitting these difficulties to a single soul. If you cry every day for the first month after your baby is born, wondering what you've done with your life, does that mean you have an 'adjustment disorder'? If you spend hours scrolling through your Instagram feed, hoping to find just one other photograph of a pregnant woman whose skin is as spotty and ankles as swollen as yours, does that mean you've developed body dysmorphia, or an Internet addiction, or both? Are your struggles pathological, or normal, or some thorny combination of the two? And if these issues are so common, then why are so many books and websites fixated with which kind of fruit your gestating fetus most closely resembles, rather than the more salient question of what might be going on with your brain as the months tick by? It's all very well to know that your baby is the size of a pomegranate, but when you can't pull your leggings over your bump without being overcome by a crushing sense of impending doom, any grocery-related niceties pale into insignificance.

In our privileged position at the sharp end of women's hopes and fears, we midwives are well placed to estimate the true extent of women's psychological struggles during the childbearing year. And I can say with absolute certainty that these challenges are poorly served by the nebulous diagnosis of 'baby brain'. That woman in your office who always has the chicest maternity clothes might be the same woman who phoned me at 2 a.m., choking out enough words to convey that she was in the grips of a terrifying panic attack – her third that week. The bolshy pregnant teenager who pushed past you at the bus stop yesterday might be the very one who appeared unannounced in Triage in the wee hours of the morning, face covered in snot and tears, begging for a bed because she was afraid of what she would do to herself if she stayed at home for a minute longer. Under that hoodie are rows of wounds razored neatly into her arms; some still raw, some already tough with silver scar tissue.

Of course, not all cases of modern-day 'baby brain' are apparent to the average observer. Some women excel at carrying secret wounds while smiling serenely at the world, but a skilled midwife can find what is hidden. She can listen, she can believe, and on the right day, she can heal.

Jaspreet:
Too Many Hours in the Day

I just couldn't work it out. Like so many of the women who end up in Triage – appearing at the desk immaculately groomed and smiling, in spite of having phoned in tears only hours before – I was beginning to wonder whether Jaspreet was one of the countless 'worried well' who keep us in such brisk business. It's not unusual for midwives to quip that a patient has been 'miraculously cured' simply by the act of arriving at the hospital. Abdominal pain that failed to respond to truckloads of paracetamol suddenly vanishes before the patient's bottom has even hit a bed; throbbing headaches mysteriously cease amid the chaotic din of the waiting room. The genuinely ill women arrive sick and stay sick until treatment is initiated, but for so many others, inhaling the hospital's heady whiff of sympathy and disinfectant seems to provide a fast fix. The more cynical among us might regard these women with a hefty dose of side-eye, and the oft-uttered assessment, 'She's at it.'

The softer among us might surmise that for so many women, the maternity hospital is a place where they know they will be listened to, and heard, and held in a safe space for an hour or an afternoon. This alone is sometimes enough to soothe and heal before the consultation has even begun.

Jaspreet – or 'Jas', as she introduced herself – had phoned the department at three o'clock on a steady day shift, when the after-lunch slump had begun to slow my step and blunt my thoughts. The morning had been awash with women whose waters had broken during the previous night's full moon, and by the afternoon my hand actually ached from doing so many examinations. Some of these patients had been admitted to the antenatal ward, some had been rushed round to labour ward, and a disgruntled few had been sent back home 'to establish', as we call it – in other words, to soak through a few packs of maternity pads and wait for the pain to come. By the time Jas called, I was a little punch-drunk from the day's workload. I had collapsed into a chair by the desk, hoping for a moment's reprieve, but the phone lit up as if on cue.

'Triage, Midwife Hazard speaking, how can I help you?' I trilled automatically.

'Well, what it is, is … I had my baby eighteen days ago and I feel tired all the time.'

I sat back and flicked my pen across the desk in jaded resignation. *Of course you're bloody tired all the time,* I wanted to say. *You can probably count on one hand the hours of solid sleep you've had since delivery, your rigid, swollen breasts are leaching every last ounce of your energy into the baby in your arms, your vagina may well be a road map of hastily sutured highways and byways, and you're wondering whether your life will ever be normal again. Of course you're tired, my love – how could you not be?*

'So, you feel tired all the time?' I enquired coolly in my best telephone voice, with exactly the right modulation of gentle concern. Mirror the patient, we're taught. Repeat back what she's told you, so she feels listened to, even if she's just confided that her labia look like rotten pork (true story).

'I'm exhausted,' said the voice down the line, 'no matter how many naps I get, or what I eat, or what I do. And my Caesarean scar is getting more and more painful every day.'

Now she had my full attention. Fatigue is hardly front-page news in a maternity hospital – for patients and staff alike – but a wound that fails to heal with good hygiene and the passage of time can indicate an infection.

'Does the area look inflamed?' I asked. 'Can you see any gaping along the line of your wound, or any blood or fluid leaking out?'

'I don't know. I've been scared to have a closer look.'

It never ceases to amaze me how many women are afraid of examining their own bodies in a medical context. We spend enough time finding fault with our thighs, arms, eyebrows or any other feature that doesn't quite match up to modern beauty standards, but when it comes to lumps, bumps and issues of a more intimate nature, too many of us shy away from any serious scrutiny. Even the caller who says, 'There's something coming out of my vagina,' often balks at the suggestion to go and have a keek in the mirror, so pre-emptively disgusted is she by what genital horrors might await. I suspect that this reluctance to look, to *really* look, at one's own body says more about social conditioning than anything else. Girls often learn from an early age that their anatomy is shamefully private, out of bounds even to themselves, only to be spoken of in hushed tones and flowery euphemisms, while a boy might play cheerily with his penis in the bath as soon as he locates it. This learned behaviour can beget years of confusion, discomfort and even inconvenience – often an hour-long trip to Triage could be saved by a sneaky peek below – but as I listened to this timid voice from afar, I knew there was no point in insisting that she inspect her scar at home.

'It's difficult to tell exactly what's happening, from what you've described to me over the phone,' I said carefully, taking her details and scribbling on the call sheet: *Vague history; patient describes tender wound but sounds generally well.* I ripped the sheet out of its book and added it to the pile of others that had accumulated on the desk that day. We'd reached the point in the afternoon when it was hardly worth keeping track of who was coming in and who had already arrived; what would be, would be.

'Why don't you pop along to the hospital, Jas,' I suggested, 'and we'll assess you as soon as we can. It's a wee bit busy at the moment,' I said, with practised understatement. In the corner of the waiting room, a woman had begun to argue vociferously with her partner over the last drumstick in the bucket of chicken they'd brought along for sustenance. *Fair play*, I thought, surveying the seven other women tutting and sighing behind the glass partition. *You could be waiting a while.*

When Jas arrived in Triage, she looked every inch the newly minted yummy mummy. She was slim, petite and neat as a pin; her glossy black hair was tied up in a perfectly spherical bun, and she'd matched her red lipstick exactly to the baby-changing bag slung over her shoulder. When I offered to carry the car seat she'd brought, her cherub sleeping peacefully in its cushioned confines, she simply smiled and lifted the seat as if it was nothing.

'I can do it myself,' she said. 'But thank you.' I had been expecting a wilting waif who could barely hold her own weight, but a calm, capable mother had come in her place. I returned Jas's smile – mirroring, always mirroring – and guided her to bed one.

Jas gently set the car seat down on the floor and sat back on the bed, swinging her feet in their box-fresh trainers up onto the sheets in one fluid movement. I regarded her with quiet scepticism as I switched on the various machines and monitors at the bedside. Few women who were only weeks post-section could have moved with such comfort and ease, let alone a woman with an abdominal infection. Jas rolled up the sleeve of her silk blouse obligingly as I wrapped the blood-pressure cuff around her arm, and she replied to my initial questions with answers that were polite but lacking in any significant detail.

'Jas,' I said, 'your observations are all normal and reassuring. Is it OK if I have a little look at your wound now? If I have any concerns, I'll ask the doctor to come and see you too.'

Jas smiled brightly. 'Of course,' she said, unzipping her jeans and wriggling them down until the waistband sat below the twin arcs of her hipbones. Her abdomen was a smooth expanse of taut, tawny skin; she was one of the few women whose luck (or, more likely, genetics) had allowed them to avoid the burst-balloon look of most new mothers. With almost no overhang to speak of, Jas's wound was easy to see: a neat red line running across her belly. I made a mental note to find out which doctor had performed the Caesarean; the even incision was the confident work of a master. Slipping on a pair of blue gloves from the bedside trolley, my fingers slid smoothly along the contours of the wound. There was no gaping, no oozing, no flap of skin 'sitting proud' of the opposing edge. Jas's scar could have graced the pages of a textbook.

I felt an embarrassing twinge of envy during this examination. My own Caesarean wound, now fifteen years old and little more than a silver seam, had been stapled instead of stitched, for some reason I'll never know or understand. For the first few weeks after my daughter's birth, I looked and felt like Frankenstein's monster – a tired, tearful, patchwork ogre. I've seen this slightly unhinged look in the eyes of so many new mothers, and for those whose labour is punctuated in the eleventh hour (or twentieth, or thirty-fourth) by an emergency Caesarean section, that sleep-deprived delirium is often exacerbated by the sting of guilt and disappointment. The hours of antenatal classes; the meticulously memorised visualisations and affirmations; the colour-coded, four-page birth plan – all end up on the cutting-room floor of the operating theatre. This mode of delivery can be life-saving, and many women are happy to embrace it as such. However, for others, the grim show-reel of this often traumatic experience plays on a loop until time renders the images grainy enough to ignore. I searched Jas's face for some sign of this inner turmoil, but her expression gave nothing away.

'Jas,' I began. 'It's totally understandable that you're exhausted all the time; your body's been through so much. You've had quite a substantial operation, which may not have been how you imagined things would go.'

She blinked at this, but resumed her steady gaze. I decided to continue; perhaps some part of my rambling monologue would hit its mark.

'You're probably surviving on a tiny amount of sleep, and it takes a huge amount of energy to meet your baby's needs. But as far as your wound goes, I can't see any obvious problems – in fact, the doctor seems to have done a beautiful job.'

She looked away then, and I thought I saw the wet gleam of a tear in one of her eyes.

'Have you been particularly active, maybe, in the last few days? A section cuts through many layers of tissue, not only the skin, so everything underneath will still be trying to heal. If you try to do too much too soon, it can feel quite painful.'

That did it. A single perfect tear slid down Jas's cheek. Her lower lip began to tremble, and then another tear followed the first, and then another, until two slick tracks made pale lines through her make-up.

'There are just too many hours in the day,' she whispered, her eyes still downcast.

I wasn't sure I'd heard her correctly. Too many hours in the day? I was unpleasantly familiar with the concept of there being too few hours – the combined demands of midwifery and parenting and general life admin had been particularly onerous of late – but too many hours?

'Sorry?' I said softly. 'What do you mean?'

Jas looked up then; her eyes were already blood-shot, and her lipstick was smudged where she had tried to wipe away a tear with the back of her hand. The mask had slipped and she was ready to talk.

'My husband was only off work for four days after Beena was born. He's self-employed, so if he doesn't work, he doesn't earn. It's OK – I don't blame him – but it's just … now that it's only me and Beena in the house for almost the whole day, time seems to drag and drag. I mean, I have to feed her, but when that's not happening, I don't know what to do with myself. I'm an accountant; I'm used to having people around me all day, being busy, going to meetings. But now there's ... all this time, and if I don't do something, I end up thinking about the birth again and again. How it went. How it should have gone. The look on my husband's face when they took me to theatre.'

I winced at this. It wasn't until years after my own Caesarean section that my husband told me what had happened after I was wheeled out of the delivery room to be prepared for surgery.

'They sent me to what was basically a broom closet to get changed,' he said one night as we lay in bed in the dark, exchanging sleepy confidences. 'I thought you and the baby were both going to die, and I had visions of myself leaving the hospital alone.' It turns out I wasn't the only one of us with a vivid inner show-reel, but my husband had kept his memories to himself until mine had begun to fade.

'I have to stop myself thinking about his face,' Jas said, echoing my thoughts. 'I have to pass the time – all those hours – so I clean.'

'You clean?' I asked. 'How much?'

Jas sniffed, took a deep, shuddering sigh, and looked me squarely in the face.

'I clean the house three or four times a day. Top to bottom. The carpets, the surfaces, the kitchen, the bathrooms. I make the beds. I sterilise Beena's bottles twice for good measure, and then I do the dishes, and then I start again.'

'So you've been ... pretty active.'

'Yes.'

I took a smaller but no less weary sigh. Suddenly I was aware of the noises behind the thin curtain that divided bed one from the rest of the room: I could hear the beats of the CTGs at the other bedsides, a man laughing and a woman snapping at him in rebuke. The phone, as ever, was ringing. I watched Jas push the damp hair back from her face, tucking a few wisps back into her shiny bun, and I wondered if I had the time, energy and insight to give her what she needed. Her emotional state was complex – a knot of anxiety, disappointment and mildly obsessive behaviours, with a slender strand of post-traumatic stress woven through the tangle, impossible to unpick in an afternoon. Hers was the conflicted, contradictory and simply scunnered brain of the average new mother.

'Jas, what you're feeling – all of it – is completely normal. Having a baby is a huge change. It's like a bomb going off in the middle of the life you had before.

Everything's different, and when you're on your own all day, it's easy to feel isolated and overwhelmed.'

She looked at me and nodded. She was obviously hearing what I was saying, but it was impossible to tell whether she was really listening. Her eyes, tearful and searching only moments before, had now begun to glaze, and I recognised that look as the very same one my teenage daughter gave me when I attempted to impart any pearls of maternal wisdom. The shutters were coming down.

'Cleaning is normal too,' I continued, hoping to reel Jas back in, 'but cleaning three or four times a day is ... maybe a bit much. Life's too short, and Beena will only ever be a baby once. Slow down. Be kind to yourself. And ask for help if you need it.'

I recognised the futility of these platitudes as soon as they left my mouth. Jas had already begun to zip up her jeans and rearrange her blouse, but it didn't feel right to give up now, to send her back to the very same situation after only a brief exchange. The midwife's art lies in knowing when a woman needs another dimension to her care, and I sensed that for Jas, words – or at least, the clumsy assurances I had offered – would not be enough. I knew there were only seconds until she retreated back to the lonely world she'd come from, folding her sadness and her baby to her breast. And then it came to me.

'Jas,' I said as she lowered her feet back down to the floor. She paused and looked at me, waiting to see what more, if anything, I had to offer. 'I think there is actually something I can do for your wound.'

She tilted her chin; the gesture was perfunctory, birdlike; a cursory invitation to elaborate.

'You've been so active that, on second thoughts, there might well be some low-grade inflammation below your suture line.' I was flannelling wildly, but it seemed to be working. Jas stilled as she listened to my 'diagnosis'.

'I'd like to give your wound an antimicrobial soak, to soothe the scar and reduce any harmful bacteria. It will only take ten minutes, and all you have to do is lie back and relax. Beena will be fine.' I glanced at the child snuffling dreamily in her car seat amid the raucous lullaby of Triage.

'I suppose I could stay,' Jas said, 'if you really think there's something that will help.'

'Absolutely,' I replied, smiling. What I had in mind would have minimal clinical effect – in essence, it was little more than a wash and a rest – but I knew that the 'treatment' would certainly do no harm. I could avail myself of any instrument or drug that modern obstetrics might have to offer, but in this case, suggestion and intent were likely to be much more powerful.

I reached into a drawer at the bedside and laid out my materials on the top of the trolley: sterile gloves, two packets of gauze swabs, and a long plastic ampoule of wound-cleansing fluid. Performance has its own role to play in midwifery, and I felt Jas looking on with interest as I opened each pack. She lifted her top and undid her jeans once more, and tenderly, slowly, with a very deliberate sense of ceremony, I unfolded the ten cotton squares and laid them side by side along the line of her scar. When the wound was finally covered in a swathe of clean white gauze, I snapped open the ampoule and trickled its contents over the makeshift bandages until each thread of the fabric was saturated. Whenever I dress a wound in this way, I remember that this is an act of loving validation; every wound tells a story, and every dressing is an acknowledgement of that story – the midwife's way of saying, *I hear you, and I believe you.*

'There,' I said, patting down each swab with the lightest of touches. 'We'll let that sink in now. I'll pop out for a few minutes. You rest.' I dimmed the light above Jas's bed before I left the bay. As I drew the curtain, I saw her lying back with her eyes closed and her arms at her sides. The rise and fall of her belly was just visible beneath the layer of wet swabs. In this small corner of Triage, there was peace.

I passed a quick ten minutes shuttling between the phone and the growing heap of incoming patients' case notes. As I answered a call about a thirty-one-weeker in preterm labour and another from a woman who was sitting in a small pool of blood on the bus home from work, I was increasingly aware of the need to clear some beds for these and any other urgent cases that the early-evening rush might bring. I gave Jas as much of a rest as I could before returning to her bed space, where I found her snoring softly. Her hands still lay at her sides, but as sleep had come, her palms had turned upwards as if in supplication.

'Jas,' I said, kneeling to give her shoulder a gentle shake. 'How are you feeling?'

She opened her eyes. There was a moment while she registered this strange face, and the even stranger surroundings. 'I'm OK,' she said. She looked down at her belly and peeled back an edge of wet gauze. 'This felt good. Thank you.'

It felt good to me too, I wanted to say. The hospital seemed to be growing busier by the day; too many of my shifts had been passing in a frantic blur, and I was aware that my touch had become less gentle and my intention less clear. As older colleagues took early retirement or left to pursue less stressful jobs, younger midwives had flooded in, then quickly balked at the realities of life on the wards. This had left me sandwiched uncomfortably in the middle – not senior enough to know all the ropes, or junior enough to be given the benefit of the doubt if things went wrong. It was an uneasy feeling, and I struggled at times to see where I fitted into the system, and whether my presence was making a difference. To know, though, that I could still offer comfort, and could give a woman ten minutes of precious pause – this did feel good.

Jas put herself together with practised efficiency; jeans up once more, shirt tucked, wet gauze folded in a neat pile at the bedside. She wouldn't let me lift

Beena's car seat, nor would she accept my offer of clean swabs and painkillers for the road. I walked with her to the double doors of the department and watched her stride away with that same easy grace I'd noticed on her arrival. There were still many hours left in her day – and in mine – and we would both continue to bear our wounds as we worked; Jas with her cloth and spray, me with my gloves and gauze, each ploughing our own furrow of healing and pain.

Notes on the Uniform

A starched white dress, a fob watch dangling from a polished chain, a wide elastic belt cinched with a silver filigree clasp. Opaque tights, neatly laced shoes tied with identical double knots. The picture of a proud, efficient midwife. This was never me, although I often fantasise about the uniform I missed out on by twenty years, before the powers-that-be decided that staff would be much more productive (and cheaper to clothe) if they wore unisex tunics and trousers. The stiff-winged caps, the *Call the Midwife* capes: these were out, and a gender-neutral two-piece was in. This, we were told, was progress.

My cohort of students were the first to be given the new, nationally decreed uniform. Regardless of the undeniable ugliness of the clothes, we rushed as a giggling mass into the classroom that had become our designated fitting room on a Friday a few months into our training. With its desks pushed to the walls and its wide windows looking out onto the bleak cityscape beyond, the room was freezing. Still, we couldn't wait to strip off and try on our freshly starched uniforms ahead of being let loose on our first clinical placements. Although we howled at each other in our ashen-grey tunics and navy drawstring cargo trousers, there was no mistaking the pride we felt as we twirled and posed, enjoying the strange thrill of the stiff fabric against our goose-pimpled skin. We were a ragtag bunch, ranging in age from seventeen to forty-one years old, some living away from home for the first time, others balancing classwork with young families. Some of us were still plagued with acne, while others bemoaned grey hairs and grumpy teenagers, but for the first time, our uniforms made us just that: uniform; the same. We had walked different paths, but we delighted in our new, shared identity. Finally, we looked the part.

As we would come to realise over the following weeks, a uniform is both an identifier and a cloak of invisibility. It allows the wearer to be seen as official, knowledgeable, respectable; and in doing so, it also allows them to slip without question or reproach into environments where someone in 'civvy' clothes would instantly stand out as an unwanted, even potentially dangerous, intruder. Roaming a ward for the first time, asking a total stranger if you can check her stitches: of course! (Cue sheet being drawn up, and knees dropping swiftly open to reveal the fresh aftermath of a forceps delivery.) Pressing the buzzer to a fifteenth-floor flat, and being met with the scowling figure of a seven-foot giant and his growling Rottweiler: Come in, sister, he won't bite! (Cue the giant falling over himself to bring you tea and custard creams while you examine his girlfriend's flushed, swollen breasts.) With each shift, we began to inhabit our uniforms and our world with greater confidence, and as we edged further into the throbbing heart of the hospital, we swapped our grey tunics for scrubs. This had the phenomenal effect of rendering us completely indistinguishable from the qualified midwives and doctors who worked alongside us – until, of course, we opened our mouths.

I was in the middle of my second year of training when an opportunity arose to observe a day of gynae-cological outpatient surgery. Although I had started to feel slightly less of a bumbling rookie, this smaller hospital was completely new to me, and even the thought of entering the theatres here filled me with panic. In my few stints assisting with Caesarean sections, I had been unable to shake the strong feeling of being completely, relentlessly, in everyone's way. There were so many rituals and rules – touch this, don't touch that, stand here but not there – that I feared I would never be at home in the theatre, never be comfortably casual enough to swap dirty jokes and holiday plans over a woman's open abdomen, as so many of the senior midwives seemed able to do. Nevertheless, I turned up for my day of gynae surgery in my shiny new uniform, and was shown to the changing rooms by one of the staff nurses.

'This will be a quick day for you,' she said as she left me to sift through the usual bins of oversized scrubs. 'Dr Munn fires through them on a Thursday so she can pick up her kids from nursery. Blink and you'll miss it,' she said with a wink, and she turned on the heel of her neon-pink Crocs.

True to the nurse's promise, the day got off to a flying start. In the cavernous theatre, bright lamps glinting off chrome trolleys and gleaming floors, the various staff – anaesthetist, nurses, assistants and auxiliaries – gathered for the start of the show. At one minute past nine, Dr Munn appeared in her scrubs, gloved hands held aloft to avoid contamination, and her flinty blue eyes danced behind her glasses as she announced to the waiting crowd, 'Keep up, guys and gals. We'll be out of here by three.' I hung back against the wall, spectating from a safe distance while the day's first case was wheeled in. She was young, and already anaesthetised, and I watched goggle-eyed as the doctor powered up her suction and quickly removed what remained of a missed miscarriage from the patient's uterus. Job done, patient out. Next: an older woman with a cyst. Trolley in, cyst out, wound closed, patient out. I crept closer and closer to the operating table as the day went on, until finally the last person on the list was brought in: a woman in her mid-thirties with endometriosis. It was to be a laparoscopic procedure, where Dr Munn would slide a camera and any other necessary instruments through keyhole incisions in the patient's abdomen, and blast away the offending tissue.

With the same brisk efficiency I had now come to expect, Dr Munn approached the operating table for the sixth time that day, opened the patient's belly and plunged the camera inside. As the doctor's arm lunged and swung, moving the laparoscope here and there, her eyes remained firmly fixed on a nearby screen, where the patient's internal organs were projected in vivid close-up. There was a glimpse of the smooth, pink uterus, suffused with tiny thread-like veins; a flash of the ovaries, like polished almonds; and then a longer look at the wayward fragments of endometrial tissue, small anemones that seemed to vaporise under the ministrations of Dr Munn's mini blowtorch. After only a few minutes of this pelvic slash-and-burn, Dr Munn nodded at the screen, satisfied with her handiwork, and then she peered at me for the first time over the sleek chrome frames of her glasses. She didn't know my name or the level of my training; she hadn't asked. She'd seen the scrubs – and that was enough.

'Come on over and I'll show you a few things,' she called.

I approached the table hesitantly. How could I possibly help during this procedure? I had the basic knowledge to understand what was being done, but handling a laparoscope was completely beyond my remit.

'Hurry up now,' she said, and nodded to the space next to her at the table. As directed, I stood beside her and assumed the standard pose of the student midwife: frozen with terror. The patient lay in front of us: green-draped, eyes closed, hair spread out on the black vinyl of the table, tongue lolling beside the airway tubing that was keeping her alive while the anaesthetic suspended her body in a shroud of sleep.

Dr Munn nodded towards the screen. 'Let's have a look around,' she said, as casually as if she were inviting me into her home. 'See what we can find.' My panic subsided rapidly when I realised that, far from expecting me to operate the camera, Dr Munn was about to give me a guided tour of human anatomy. While the procedure itself had been quick, with the doctor moving the instruments deftly from one area to the next, now she worked slowly and demonstratively for my benefit, and as if by magic, the screen revealed an easily identifiable wedge of smooth tissue.

'Her liver,' Dr Munn commented. And then, another leisurely sweep, and a bundle of fleshy rope. 'Her intestine.' Sweep again; the movement was almost balletic. 'Her uterus, and the fallopian tubes. These are ligaments,' she said, pointing to taut, fleshy cords, 'and these are the ureters.' And so on. My eyes were riveted to the screen. As I stood there sweating under the theatre lights, the clock on the wall ticking towards

3 p.m., I marvelled at the madness of the moment. With only my scrubs as my passport, I had been invited on a journey through the internal geography of a stranger's body, the fleshy, throbbing landmarks both exotic and familiar. There was little difference between me and the people milling around the hospital café on the other side of the theatre walls in their T-shirts and jeans – and my clinical knowledge at this point was only marginally superior to theirs – but in the simple act of donning a uniform, I had been welcomed into what felt like medicine's inner sanctum.

A few years after that afternoon in theatre, I completed my training and was allowed to collect the cornflower-blue uniform of a registered midwife from a stuffy storeroom in the basement of another nearby hospital. By this time, I had caught seventy-six babies, looked after countless more women, and was slightly less mystified by the workings of the human body, but midwifery was no less magical to me than it had been on the first day of my training. If anything, my pride at slipping on the blue uniform for the first time was magnified a hundredfold from the buzz I had felt when I had received the student's grey tunic. Once again, there was the overwhelming joy and disbelief at finally 'looking the part', but this time, there was also delight in *being* the part.

As my clinical practice progressed in the first few years after I qualified, I wore the blue uniform in clinics, wards and busy treatment rooms aplenty. The chest became frayed where I pinned my name badge and fob watch day after night after day; the knees of the trousers became baggy from kneeling behind women as they squatted out their babies and from bending beside a bed to help latch a fractious baby to its mother's breast. Not every patient was delighted to see me – one labourer spat a crumbling tooth in my direction when I didn't get her diamorphine quite as quickly as she would have liked – but there was no denying that wherever I was, the uniform marked me out as someone who had earned her stripes. Even when women were doubled in pain, or rigid with fear, there was an understanding that this midwife was on their side.

I may not have had the dress of my dreams, with its starched collars and silver-buckled belt, but the uniform was my way of telling the world that I was there to serve. There was only one instance where the uniform had the opposite effect; marking me out as a threat; even as the enemy. And no polished shoes could put a shine on the darkness of that experience. Suddenly my passport to respectability was gone: I was stateless, pointless, nothing more than a woman telling another woman to put her faith, and her life, in my hands.

Star:
Meeting the Enemy

I arrived at work knowing that everyone hated me.

It wasn't my imagination; I had read it in a newspaper.

I was sitting at my kitchen table, bolting down a bowl of leftover chilli in an attempt to fill my belly before what would undoubtedly be a busy night shift in the labour ward. I had been struggling with a stomach bug, and my guts churned audibly as I shovelled the food into my mouth, contemplating the grim possibilities of what the night might bring. I'd been doing a few extra shifts in the labour ward to bulk out my pay cheque, and in spite of my best efforts, my last few patients had ended up in theatre. One for a crash section (with the patient calling the staff all the bloody bastards under the sun right up until her last moment of consciousness); one for a trial of forceps that had morphed into a Caesarean (but only after the doctor realised that he had used his huge silver salad spoons to rotate the baby from a favourable fit to a hopeless malposition, instead of the other way around); and one for a postpartum haemorrhage that had resulted in the patient's womb being removed as a last-ditch, desperate attempt to stop the bleeding at source. In short, I had had a few rough days at the office, and I was in need of some light relief.

As my stomach heaved in protest against the food I was forcing inside, I flicked through a newspaper that my husband had left before taking the girls to their evening ballet and hockey practices. (Another mark of my 'failure' as a shift-working mother: I'd been at the hospital so much that my children had stopped asking me if I could drive them to their various classes and clubs, knowing full well that the answer would always be a guilt-stricken no.) I scanned the day's headlines, hoping to come across a bit of good news to cheer me up, or even a fluff piece about a panda being born or a cat rescued from a well.

My eyes were drawn, though, to an article about the maternity services. Apparently, a recent survey had revealed a large jump in the numbers of women who reported feeling abandoned, neglected and ignored in labour. The author wrote of women who had been sent away from their local Triage unit in agonising pain, having been told that their distress was an over-reaction to the niggles of early labour. Some of these women had gone on to deliver at home or in roadside lay-bys, while other women (who had managed to achieve admission to the wards) spoke with sadness about their experiences of begging fruitlessly for painkillers as their contractions increased. Some had been left alone while they bled; others ruefully recalled the midwives who had mocked their distress. The comments ranged from the wistful – 'I wish things had been different' – to the outraged, with one woman going as far as to call all midwives 'a bunch of cruel, twisted gatekeepers'.

So there it was. In spite of the hundreds of hours of exhausting toil, in spite of the fact that so many of the midwives I knew had sacrificed their time, their sleep, their physical and mental health, and their most precious personal relationships in the name of their career, we were hated. I knew first-hand the difficulty of assessing a labourer in the knowledge that there were no beds for her anywhere in the hospital, regardless of the result of my examination. I knew what it was like to have to send a woman home, assuring her through gritted teeth that 'a couple of paracetamol and a hot bath will see you through the next few hours'. I knew how it felt to bounce around an ante-natal ward like a demented pogo stick in midwife's clothing, trying in vain to care for six different patients at once, apologising to one about the shortage of birth balls, assuring another that I would get her diamorphine as soon as my other, equally manic colleague was free to check it with me, and placating the rest with rushed words of comfort and a rictus grin.

I had missed birthday parties and school concerts. I had reduced my relationship with my husband to a mumbled 'hello' when I tumbled into bed after a night shift as he was getting up to make the children's packed lunches. I had dragged myself into the hospital with heavy colds and dodgy tummies that I'd probably picked up – guess where – in the hospital, a kind of presenteeism fuelled only by copious amounts of coffee and a deep-seated fear of letting my colleagues down. All this was true, but still we were hated, and here in front of me was the undeniable proof.

I pushed away the half-eaten chilli, along with the newspaper and the pint of Diet Coke I had poured in an attempt to mainline some caffeine before my shift.

It was 6.45 p.m., and cruel, twisted gatekeeper or not, I was a midwife with a job to do; somewhere on the other side of the city was a woman who was waiting for my care. I bundled my bags and myself into the car and drove through the balmy June evening, passing families picnicking in the park and beautiful young things flirting in the sun outside cafés and bars. I wondered – not for the first time, or the last – why I was rushing to spend twelve and a quarter hours shut in a windowless room with a stranger, instead of relaxing with my husband and a chilled glass of wine in the garden. Even as I contemplated this parallel universe, where I had a normal job and did normal things, my brain drove me to the hospital on autopilot. As I pulled into the car park, I prayed only for an easy night with a pleasant patient who might enjoy my company (and, ideally, not end up flat on her back in theatre while a doctor raked clot after clot from her exhausted, atonic uterus).

An hour later, it seemed as though my prayers may have been answered. The nightly lottery in the labour suite's bunker had allocated me a low-risk, twenty-six-year-old woman who was already eight centimetres dilated with her first baby. As I entered her room, I could feel the tension drain from my body.

The atmosphere was almost soporifically relaxing; the lights were dimmed, Ibiza-style chill-out music thrummed softly from the stereo in the corner, and the air was heavy with the scent of lavender and clary sage. This was one of the hospital's few rooms with a birth pool, and my patient was making full use of the large oval tub. She reclined against the side, eyes closed, smiling with Buddha-like serenity as her tumble of purple-tipped dreadlocks dipped and swirled in the water lapping at her cleavage. She was unabashedly naked, and her long, lean body was covered in elaborate tattoos of flowering vines and branches; her ears pierced with a glittering array of studs, safety pins and coloured discs. Behind her knelt a man who was very clearly her 'other half' on every level, so closely did his appearance and energy match hers. He had a dreadlocked topknot, a solemn face, and equally bedazzled ears; the tangle of scuffed silver chains around his neck jangled softly as he leaned over his lady and massaged her shoulders with strong, spindly fingers. As he moved, she swayed gently in the water, sending ripples across the surface of the pool. They were one, they were in the Zone. This would be easy.

I didn't recognise the young midwife who was scribbling some final notes at the worktop in the corner. She was part of the influx of newly qualified girls required to fill the gaps left by an exodus of burnt-out, hacked-off senior staff who had run for the hills. This one looked like she was barely out of school, with a button nose and a downy softness to her cheeks that only added to the impression of youth. She finished her writing and stared at the notes in consternation.

'I hope I haven't forgotten anything,' she said apologetically as she went to leave the room. 'Anyway, they're lovely. Star and Moss. You'll have a good night.' She smiled, and left.

Star's head lolled onto her chest and she began to inhale deeply through her nose, blowing back out across the water with a long, low sigh. As a contraction rolled through her body, Moss's fingers travelled down Star's arms, and he grasped her firmly, steadying her with his grip, until the pain eased off and her breath softened again.

'All good, babe, all good,' he murmured as her body relaxed and his fingers resumed their hypnotic knead and pull. She opened her eyes for the first time and lifted her face to Moss; they beamed at each other, and he planted a soft kiss on her forehead. If they knew that I was in the room, they weren't showing it.

I crept over to the pool and knelt beside it. 'Hey,' I ventured.

Star and Moss looked over to me, seeming to register my presence for the first time.

'Hey,' they both replied in distant, blissed-out voices. Star squinted as she realised I was a different person from the midwife who'd been with them all day.

'Are you going to catch my baby?' she asked.

I smiled. 'Hopefully, you'll catch your own baby. If you deliver in the pool, that's pretty much how it happens. I'll be hands-off if all goes well.'

'Cool,' Star said, beaming. 'Very cool.' She closed her eyes again and leaned back into Moss's embrace.

'It looks like these contractions are nice and strong,' I said.

'We'd prefer to call them surges,' Moss said as his fingers worked the knots at Star's vine-strewn shoulders. 'We're Hypnobirthing. We're going to breathe this baby out, aren't we, babe?'

Star smiled, eyes still closed, and she began a soft, low hum as another 'surge' rumbled across her belly. It had been ages since I'd had a low-risk, or 'Green Pathway', patient, and I was so ready for this cosmically relaxed couple; they were just doing their thing. Prior to becoming a midwife, I had been lucky enough to attend a few home births as a spectator and supporter. The vibe in the labour room that night took me straight back to those early experiences, when birth was a celebration, yes, but also simply another event in the life of the family: babies arriving in pools, or baths, or in candlelit nests of cushions and quilts, with friends and siblings crying happy tears over tea and home-baked cakes. The heady fug of essential oils was both exotic and familiar, and I could feel myself drift easily into the mood that Star and Moss had already created, oblivious to the alarms and emergencies of the labour ward outside the door.

When the surge had passed, I asked Star if I could listen to her baby and check her vital signs. She murmured her consent, draping one arm over the edge of the pool so I could strap on the Velcro cuff, and bobbing her belly helpfully to the water's surface to allow me to listen in. I pressed my handheld Doppler to her bump and found the baby's heartbeat just above her pubic bone; the sound was steady and clear, and at 140 beats per minute, it sat reassuringly in the middle of the normal range.

19.52, I wrote in Star's labour and birth notes, picking up where the day-shift midwife had left off. *Observations normal, Star breathing through uterine activity 3 in 10 minutes, moderate to strong on palpation. Plan: low-risk care, intermittent auscultation of the fetal heart, vaginal examination at 23.30 if no signs of imminent delivery, or sooner if indicated.* So far, so good, I thought as I slipped my pen back into my pocket and admired the harmonious scene in front of me.

We passed the next few hours in this way, settling into an easy rhythm. I lingered by the side of the tub, doing my checks and observations as silently and unobtrusively as possible in between Star's surges, then retreated as soon as I heard her breath deepen and saw Moss's grip tighten on her arms. Now and again, she would change position, stretching her legs out in front of her, or drifting onto all fours while Moss scooped handfuls of warm water over the rising-sun tattoo that covered her lower back. I could see strands of blood-streaked mucus or 'show' drifting around her ankles as she shifted in the water. This was a good omen: a sign that the neck of the womb was loosening, releasing the plug that had sealed it for the last forty-one weeks. Star was unaware as I scooped these jelly-like strands away and topped up the pool with fresh water; she swayed and rocked through her surges, eyes closed, swimming through an inner cosmos where even Moss couldn't join her.

22.58, I wrote in the notes at my side. *Patient coping well, enjoying benefit of pool and support of partner Moss. Uterine activity now 4 in 10 minutes. Copious show visible per vaginam.*

At first, there were only subtle signs that the mood had shifted. Star begin to flinch and squirm under Moss's touch. Instead of allowing him to hold her through her surges, she drifted towards the middle of the pool, unreachable, an island. Her dreadlocks fanned around her as she breathed and heaved through ever more powerful contractions. Moss sat back on his heels by the side of the tub and continued his chant of 'Well done, babe, all good, babe,' as each surge passed. Star responded with only the hint of a smile, then stopped responding completely, then grimaced when he spoke, his words a hollow echo to the pain that was now tearing through her body. It had been over four hours since Star had been examined by the day-shift midwife, and although I didn't want to interrupt her flow, instinct and protocol both told me that it would be wise to know whether her cervix was continuing to open and labour was progressing.

'Star,' I said, in between contractions, 'I'm going to check your pulse, temperature and blood pressure, and then if it's OK with you, I'd like to do a gentle internal examination. It's been a while since you were checked, and it's really helpful to know whether things are moving on. I'll be as quick as I can, and then if everything's all right, we can keep on doing what we're doing.'

She opened her eyes enough to peer at me through narrow slits. Her cheeks were flushed, and wispy hairs had worked themselves loose from her dreadlocks and lay plastered by sweat to her forehead. 'Will I have to leave the pool?' she asked. Her voice was reedy and ragged from hours of heavy breathing.

'I'll do these observations first – you can stay where you are – but then yes, you'll have to get out for a little while. It's really hard to do an accurate examination under water, but being up and about could do you some good anyway. We might even get you along to the toilet; emptying your bladder could give the baby's head more room to come down.'

She pressed her eyes shut while I bustled about her with my blood-pressure machine and my thermometer, hurrying to do my bits and pieces before the next contraction came. Her blood pressure was fine, but her pulse was elevated at 123 beats per minute, and her temperature was 38.1 degrees Celsius, well above the upper limit of normal. As I pressed my Doppler to her belly, her baby's heartbeat raced loudly in response: 178 beats per minute, with no sign of easing up. I frowned as I jotted down my observations, water from my hands dripping onto the page like teardrops: *23.34: Maternal tachycardia and pyrexia noted; fetal tachycardia with reduced beat-to-beat variability*. Either Star was overheating in the pool, or her labour was showing signs of obstruction, or she was brewing an infection, or any combination of the three. None of it was good for her baby, and whatever was going on, I needed to get a few things done.

'Star,' I began. Her eyes were still tight, and she was breathing faster now, her shoulders visibly shaking as another surge began. Moss hung back at the opposite side of the pool, a look of helpless bewilderment on his face. 'Star, your pulse and temperature are high, and your baby's heartbeat is a lot faster than I'd like. I think it would be a really good idea to check where we're at now. Let's see if we can cool you down, maybe try some paracetamol to lower your temperature, maybe pop your baby on the continuous monitor to keep a closer eye on things.' I flinched at hearing myself use the midwife's verbal tic of trivialising interventions – 'pop' you on the monitor, 'pop' up on the bed, put a 'wee' clip on the baby's head – but I was worried, and the luxuries of time and careful word choice had abandoned me.

'Don't fucking touch me,' a voice growled. The tone was so brutal, so hateful, I had to do a double-take to confirm that it was Star who had spoken. Her face contorted as another contraction arrived hot on the heels of the last, and she threw back her head and moaned in raw, unmistakeable pain.

'It's OK, babe,' Moss said, 'you're still the boss.' He reached across the water towards Star, but she batted his hand away, and he retreated, shocked, into the shadows.

'And you can fucking get to fuck as well,' she spat, before another ripple of pain passed through her, and she clawed at her scarlet cheeks. I had often seen women become desperate, foul-mouthed and even aggressive during the 'transition' phase of labour that precedes active pushing. Patients swearing at me or at their partners was nothing new; sometimes, the sight of a woman losing it a bit can even be an encouraging sign that the contractions are strong, and birth will be imminent. A midwife would be churlish to take offence at this normal response; her skill lies in keeping calm while guiding the woman through her personal storm. This was something else, though; there was an undertone of bile to Star's voice that caught me off-guard.

'Star ...' I said again. 'I want to keep you safe, and keep your baby safe, but I can only do that if you let me.'

'Don't touch me!' she shouted, her eyes flying open. And then, just as quickly, she squeezed her eyes closed and curled into a ball in the middle of the pool, the water lapping around her shoulders as she began a frantic incantation. 'Don't touch me don't touch me don't touch me don't touch me,' she babbled, until the words melted together into a tumble of incoherence and gave way to a bone-splitting groan. Her hands searched for the side of the pool, and as she grasped the rim with claw-like, white-knuckled hands, I seized the opportunity to slide two fingers gently under her left wrist to re-check her pulse. It was 129 beats per minute now, I estimated, before she whipped her hand away and fixed me with a wild glare.

'I told you not to fucking touch me!' she roared.

'Please, Star, I'm worried about you ...'

'You're just like all the rest. I knew it! All you want is for me to lie on my back so you can stick your hand in me. And I'm not doing it.' With a splash, she stood bolt upright in the pool, water running down her naked body in a hundred tiny rivers. Her enormous belly seemed to glisten and throb as she towered over Moss and me. 'Well, guess what: it's not happening,' she screamed. 'Because I'm out of here. I'm leaving. I'll deliver this baby my fucking self if I have to, by the side of the fucking road. Gaaaaaggggh,' she moaned, and doubled over with her hands on her knees as another contraction caused her bump to tighten and heave. I thought I could hear the telltale grunt of a push at the end of Star's cry, but in the current state of stalemate, there was no way I could tell for sure whether she was entering the second, expulsive stage of labour. *23.46: Patient declines to be examined,* I scribbled in the notes at my side. *Patient states she wishes to leave the hospital. Distressed+++.*

As the contraction eased, Star drew herself up again and heaved a leg over the side of the pool, splashing water onto my scrubs and across the floor. The other leg followed, and soon Star was lunging around the room, ricocheting off trolleys and walls as her rant continued.

'I'm going to get my stuff and go before you lay another hand on me,' she said, almost growling as she grabbed at the pile of overstuffed rucksacks in the corner of the room. 'Just you fucking watch, ggggnnn,' she groaned with a definite push in her voice. Moss watched, agog, lost for words.

I stood at one side of the bed, Star at the other. We were locked in a face-off. She clutched at the crisp white sheets, wide-eyed, flushed. I could feel my own cheeks burning and was suddenly aware of the heat of the room; clouds of steam billowed off the water in the pool and collected at the back of my neck in a clammy film. Even Star seemed to be radiating her own waves of angry heat, and as she stared me down, I tried desperately to match her energy with my own. I wanted only to help this woman, to do my job, to check a few things and make the best possible plan, but I could do nothing without her consent. Anything else would be assault – the very thing she was already convinced was about to happen to her. In my head, I was one of the good guys: sympathetic, open to any and all birth choices and behaviours, from the hippiest of home birthers to the divas who demanded their own private anaesthetist on speed-dial. Even on my toughest shifts, I was ready to give love to the women in my care. I could help them if they'd let me: it's the tacit midwife–patient contract that keeps the wheels of the system spinning. In Star's eyes, though, I was the enemy. There was no peace to be brokered, no love to be lost.

'Star,' I began. 'I became a midwife to help women, not to hurt them.'

She snarled, unflinching, across the bed.

'I'm a good person,' I said, pleading now, and as those words hung in the humid air, I was aware how feeble, how wheedling and insincere I must sound. But I was tired, and scared, and even a little bit angry.

'I'm on your team,' I insisted. 'Yes, there are midwives who would happily strap you up with every drip and wire you can think of. There are midwives who would examine you even if you were crying. But I'm not that midwife,' I said, as much to myself as to Star. 'I'm not the enemy.'

Before she could reply, another contraction gripped Star's body. She roared so loudly that the walls of the room seemed to shake, and as she dipped her head and gripped desperate fistfuls of the sheets on the bed between us, I could see a sliver of a golden, fluid-filled balloon protruding between her legs: the amniotic sac, the baby's watery home. My heart leapt. Star was close to delivering, although I could only guess at whether her baby would be in good condition when it came.

Star seemed to sense that something had changed. She looked up at me as the contraction died away; her eyes were softer, and her voice was different, smaller, child-like.

'What was that?' she asked.

'It's your bag of waters, Star. Your baby can't be far away.'

Silently, she paced over to the pool and heaved herself back into the water with a splash. Moss and I drew closer; he stared in anticipation at the apex of Star's legs while I started running the taps. Star might not let me touch her, but the least I could do was bring the pool back up to a safe temperature for birth.

23.50, I wrote. *Amniotic sac visible. Patient returned to pool.* Another push came, and another, and Star withdrew deeper and deeper into the inner space in her mind as the water in the pool clouded with a silent pop of straw-coloured amniotic fluid. *23.54, spontaneous rupture of membranes, clear liquor seen*, I scribbled, and I reached over and pressed the buzzer for another midwife to be present for the delivery. This was common practice in my unit: one midwife for the mother and one for the baby, in case both needed urgent attention simultaneously. I had no idea who would appear at the door, but I was grateful to have an excuse to call for backup.

Star was on all fours with her head and arms resting against the side of the pool, her rump towards me, her legs open enough to reveal a slender patch of her baby's head. It was crucial at this point that she listened to my guidance, and I began to speak as gently as possible, bracing myself for the backlash.

'It's very important that you keep your bottom either completely above or completely below the water, Star,' I said. 'If the baby feels the cold air on its body while its head is submerged, it might gasp and breathe in the pool water.'

Silently, she lowered her bottom below the water's surface.

Emboldened by her cooperation, I kept talking, my voice soft but steady: 'Do what your body is telling you – push when you need to push, and when you feel all of your baby's head stretching you open down below, just breathe.'

'That's it, babe,' Moss added quietly, cautiously. 'Breathe the baby out, just like we talked about.'

The water rippled as Star tossed her dreadlocks back in a smooth arc and girded herself for another contraction. This time, I could actually see the smooth diamond of her tailbone kicking out beneath her skin, a sure sign that the baby was moving through her pelvis. Star screamed and pushed, and as she did so, the door flew open against the wall with a bang and Mary Jane, the sister in charge, marched into the room.

'What are you doing to this poor girl? I've never heard such a racket in my life.' And then, under her voice, as the cloud of lavender and clary sage enveloped her, 'Bloody hell, it smells like a whore's drawers in here.'

'Just having a baby, sister,' I replied. As if on cue, Star reared up to a kneeling position, threw her head back, and with her lips pursed into a perfect 'O', she let out a long, low 'hooooooooooo' of breath. As she did so, her baby's head slipped out from between her legs, eyes closed, rosebud lips pursed, skin still dusky in its last moments of suspended animation. *23.59, head delivered.* Star looked down through the rippling water, saw what was there, and pushed. In a final burst of blood and liquor, her baby's body shot out, tethered only by its long, spiralling cord. Star sank further into the pool as she reached down and brought the infant up onto her chest, its body warm below the surface, its eyes now wide and blinking in the shock of the air above. A discreet glance confirmed what I thought I had seen: Star had birthed a girl. *00.01, spontaneous vaginal delivery of live female.* I began to write the next words, *Cried at birth*, automatically, then paused and set down my pen. The room was silent.

'It's purple,' Moss said, a quiver of panic in his voice. 'Why is it purple?'

The baby's skin was mottled and dusky in places. It was a familiar sight to me, but understandably worrying to someone who might only ever have seen the impossibly rosy-cheeked newborns of TV and cinema lore.

'Water babies take a bit longer to pink up,' I said. This was true, but with my luck, I thought morosely, this will be the one baby that needs resuscitation. I'll need to go through the frantic routine of inflation breaths and chest compressions that I last practised on a rubber doll six months ago, and God only knows what will happen next, and then Star's idea of me as the Devil incarnate will be well and truly confirmed. As the reel of a million different catastrophic scenarios ran through my mind, the baby opened its mouth, blew a cluster of glossy bubbles, and cried. As she bawled, a slow bloom of pink began to spread outwards from her chest to her face and her limbs. Star and Moss began to cry as well: Star with hot, silent tears, Moss with loud, racking gasps of relief. She collapsed back into his body, the baby still clasped to her breast, and Moss enveloped them both in his long, sinewy arms. The circle was complete again; Moss, Star and their baby were one.

'Well,' Mary Jane said from behind me. 'Looks like you have everything in order. Try and keep the noise down, Midwife Hazard,' she said with a wry smile, and left the room.

I had been squatting by the side of the pool, but as the door slammed shut behind Mary Jane, I allowed relief and exhaustion to tip me back onto my heels. I sat on the floor, adrift in a mess of puddles and soggy towels, my scrubs soaked with water, steam and sweat, and I watched as Star and Moss welcomed this new life to the world.

'Heyyy, baby Luna,' Moss cooed, and Star covered the baby's curled, wet hair with kisses.

'Who's my gorgeous girl,' she murmured. 'Who's my gorgeous, gorgeous girl.'

Apart from the baby, the scene was almost identical to the one that had greeted me at the start of the night: the love in the room was as heady as the fragrant oils that still drifted in dappled slicks across the surface of the pool. I wondered whether Star's outburst had even happened, or whether I had imagined its intensity, my emotions heightened by fatigue, my brain scrambled by too many hours of hard work and lost sleep. Mary Jane wouldn't even be able to corroborate the story – Sod's Law, she had arrived just as Luna slid smoothly into the pool, and she was probably already telling the rest of the staff how Midwife Hazard had been making her perfectly pleasant patient scream the house down for no good reason at all.

I dragged myself upright and shuffled over to the case notes that lay scattered across the worktop in the corner. I scanned the pages for any clues in Star's history that might help explain her outburst. I had seen situations where previous trauma or abuse lay buried in a woman until the pain of labour brought memories vividly back to life – women who flinched with fear before I'd even touched them, or whose bodies went oddly limp, their numb gaze fixed on a distant point during every examination. I remembered Star's accusation that I was 'just like all the rest', but as I read page after page of routine antenatal check-ups, there was nothing here out of the ordinary – or at least, nothing that had been disclosed. It was a mystery and, like so many women's stories, it would remain so.

Luna's cries had settled into contented gurgles and squeaks as she nuzzled into her mother's breast. Star shook her head, looked up at me and blinked, as if suddenly remembering who I was. But instead of anger, there was only love in her eyes. Her pupils were huge; she was high on birth.

'Hey,' she called to me. 'That was amazing. You were amazing.'

'Actually, *you* were amazing,' I replied. And I meant it.

Star brushed a stray dreadlock away from her face. 'I wasn't horrible to you, was I?' she asked. Her face shone – she was beautiful – but as she struggled to meet my gaze, I thought I saw a shadow of self-doubt, maybe even of embarrassment, cloud her expression.

'No,' I said. 'Of course not. You weren't horrible at all.'

Notes on Death

Student midwives are drip-fed death by their mentors, like children duped by their mothers into swallowing sour medicine in between spoonfuls of sweet, milky rice. The knowledge of death, the awareness that it hovers around the edges of life, is a slow, creeping thing. There is no good way to learn that babies sometimes die, and that mothers sometimes leave the hospital empty-handed, and there is no right way to teach or to learn these lessons.

Towards the end of my first year as a student midwife, I had begun to find my place in the rhythms and routines of the labour ward. My clinical skills were still limited, and I still lived in constant fear of humiliating myself by some unintentional misstep or error, but there were things that I could do relatively well, and I embraced those tasks wholeheartedly. I could love-bomb a labouring woman with such fierce enthusiasm that I would start to believe I had known her for ever. I could catch a baby whose heartbeat was strong, and whose mother could push long and hard. I could also tidy up after a delivery with increasing efficiency, which was no mean feat considering the mess of blood, fluids, drapes, sheets and instruments that were often part of even the most straightforward birth.

I was knee-deep in one such clean-up at the end of an especially busy night shift. My mentor and I had been with a woman since the start of the night, and in spite of various complications along the way, the birth itself had gone smoothly. The new parents were delighted with their first baby, a nine-pound girl who had cried, peed, pooed and fed within moments of being born, as if to say, *I'm here, I'm alive, I can do everything you expect of me.*

Leaving the mother with her baby suckling comfortably at the breast, I staggered down the corridor with an instrument tray under one arm and a bag of dirty linen in each hand. The familiar sounds of labour and its aftermath came from each room as I passed; the ward had been quiet at the start of the evening, but it looked as if the place had filled up while I'd been busy with my patient. I trundled into the sluice – a walk-in cupboard ram-packed with every wipe, pad and spray one might need to erase the bloody debris of maternity – and heaved my linen bags into a trolley. I turned around, set the instrument tray on the worktop, and was about to wash my hands when I saw a small plastic jar in the corner.

I recognised the jar as one of the containers we used to send samples to the pathology department: bits of tissue, cysts or whatnot that required further analysis. Normally, I wouldn't have given such a jar a second glance. The contents of these pots were usually unidentifiable fragments, abandoned momentarily by midwives too busy to label and send them straight away. There was no label on this specimen, and it had nothing to do with my patient; it shouldn't have concerned me. But for some reason, I picked it up, held it to the light, turned it round in my hand. And it was a baby.

Well, I say baby, though technically it was a fetus, or what is clinically called 'products of conception' when delivered before twenty-four weeks' gestation. For lack of a more nuanced name, though, I will call what I held in my hand a baby. To even the most inexperienced student midwife, the small, curled, wine-coloured creature within the jar looked like a baby – or something that was on its way to being a baby, and was perhaps very much a baby in the mind of the woman who had delivered it. I knew that such things happened in the hospital – labour was sometimes induced in women whose babies had already died inside them, or whose babies had such debilitating birth defects that they were, to use the industry parlance, 'incompatible with life'. Until now, for the junior student still grappling with the basics, a veil had remained drawn over this dark corner of midwifery.

I stood there under the bright fluorescent lights of the sluice, sweating in my oversized scrubs, holding the jar in my hand. It felt like finding an abandoned suitcase in the middle of an airport, or someone's child wandering alone along the side of a motorway. The panic, the confusion, the irrational but uncontrollable surge of furtive guilt – you've done nothing wrong, but you know you are in possession of something, of someone, that is definitely not yours.

A midwife passed by the door, walking briskly towards the storeroom. I didn't recognise her, but I held out the jar in my hand and called, 'Who does this belong to?' She looked back over her shoulder, shrugged and walked on.

Another minute passed under the lights, clutching the jar. My mentor would be expecting me back in the room, but I couldn't let this go without knowing at least whose it was. I'm not sure what I expected to do with that knowledge, or what difference it was going to make, but suddenly this baby and I were complicit in something, and I needed to know that it had an owner, a story, a mother.

The sister in charge of the labour suite that night came down the corridor from the other direction.

'Excuse me,' I said from the doorway. I held out the jar.

Sister looked at me dispassionately.

'Whose baby is this?' I asked.

She looked at me, then at the jar, then at me again. She was not impressed by my curiosity: to her mind, the situation didn't involve me and explaining it would only serve to delay her from attending to the ward's more pressing duties. I could see her composing some comment to that effect and then deciding that she couldn't even be bothered to say it. 'Probably room five's,' she replied, and carried on down the corridor.

And that was it. There were no words of reassurance, no balm for the monstrous uncertainty of the moment. I would never know who 'room five' was, or why she had delivered this tiny thing on that particular night, or whether anyone ever came back to label the jar, or to send it. The how and the why of it all remained a mystery, but I did learn one of the labour ward's most important lessons that night: that death is the twin of life, and the midwife delivers them both.

My second taste of this bitter medicine came a couple of years later, towards the very end of my training. By this time, I was proficient in more than tidying up and making the tea. I was trusted to look after most labouring women on my own, with my mentors hovering at the desk or even attending to other patients, while I found my own way through the challenges and changing rhythms of each shift. I could deal with diabetics on complex 'sliding scale' drips of glucose and insulin; I could match up the scraps of a ravaged perineum and stitch them back together with reasonable proficiency. I had even begun to tackle my nemesis, my clinical black spot: scrubbing for a Caesarean section with its dizzying array of instruments, swabs and drapes, each of which had to be organised and accounted for with exacting precision.

I was well past the forty deliveries required for professional qualification by the time the summer of my third year rolled around. It was light when I left the house at 6.45 a.m. for my day shifts; I was starting to bounce through the hospital doors with a spring in my step, my initial terror at entering the building not completely gone, but now more like a pesky but harmless dog, teeth nipping at my heels every now and again. I took that morning's first assignment in the bunker with eager anticipation: a healthy woman in labour with her second baby. Ideal.

By the afternoon, I had enjoyed hours of unadulterated midwifery pleasure: my role had been that of enthusiastic spectator, cheerleader and guide, with very little intervention required. The baby had more or less delivered itself, as they sometimes do – a long-awaited boy and a brother for the five-year-old who was waiting at home with her grandparents and a box set of *Peppa Pig* DVDs. Within an hour, the proud father had dressed his boy in a miniature version of his favourite football strip, with matching socks, mitts and hat, and the mother was reclining serenely on a tangle of sheets and towels.

There was a soft knock at the door. I glanced at the clock: almost five o'clock; maybe someone was letting me out for an early tea break.

'Be right back,' I said to my patient, who barely looked up as she snuggled her boy to her chest while the baby's dad rattled off a flurry of photos on his phone.

The corridor was cold and bright in comparison to the dim heat of the birthing room, and I blinked at the sight of Farah, one of the labour ward's most senior midwives. Farah and I had worked a handful of shifts together during my second year of training. She had been firm but kind, guiding me through a bit of tricky suturing and a few terrifying trips to theatre, but I had hardly seen her since then, and I wondered why she was waiting outside my room with a bundle of baby cardigans under her arm. The knee-jerk response of the student flashed through my mind: *I've done something wrong*, I thought. *That's it, I'm rumbled, and they've sent Farah to give me my marching papers.*

'I've just had a thirty-eight-week loss,' she said without warning or preamble.

'Oh,' I said, suddenly wrong-footed, cotton-mouthed. Was this a test?

'I know you haven't had much of a chance to do the losses yet, but it's your final placement, and … would you like to come and see him?' Her eyes softened with gentle concern, and she shifted the cardigans from one arm to the other. The elation of my patient having birthed her child moments before drained from my body; my legs felt leaden, my feet glued to the polished linoleum floor. Every student knew that by their third year they should at least have had some fleeting contact with the tragic but constant stream of women who passed through the labour suite bearing babies that had already died in utero. We knew that at some point we would be the sole carer for a woman to whom this had happened, and we also knew that it would be best to learn this heartbreaking role while still guided and sheltered by our mentors. We simultaneously dreaded and anticipated the day when we would cross this final frontier of midwifery but, for me, time and circumstance hadn't allowed for it yet. Farah's offer wasn't morbid or voyeuristic – it was a bittersweet favour, a tacit admission that here was an opportunity for me to face death, albeit briefly, under her wing.

The door to the blandly named 'Preparation Room' could only be opened by certain staff, and I hung back as Farah tapped her badge against the keypad. The door opened, and then closed behind us with a dull thud of finality as Farah and I huddled together in a room that was no bigger than a linen cupboard. My arms tingled with goosebumps; the room was freezing, fit for its sombre purpose. Farah edged forward and set the cardigans down on the worktop next to a cot I hadn't seen before. She peered inside and smoothed down the soft white blankets that were just visible over the cot's tall sides.

'He's beautiful,' she said.

Taking a deep breath, I edged closer to her and looked into the cot at the baby who lay within it, his head and body swaddled neatly. He *was* beautiful. His broad forehead was porcelain-smooth; a hundred dark eyelashes rested gently on full, round cheeks. Only his lips told the story of his arrival; they were tightly furled and purple, like the petals of a budding black tulip.

Farah placed a warm hand on my arm, but the room only seemed to grow colder.

There was nothing, and everything, to say about this boy.

'He *is* beautiful,' I whispered. I thought then of my girls; they would be getting ready for dinner, helping their father set the table, arguing over whose turn it was to take the bins out. Both had been silent at birth for a few awful moments; but then the moments had passed, and they had cried. This boy was suspended in that quiet void; crystalline, perfect, but silent. I wasn't sure I could ever be in that moment with a woman, but Farah was gently edging me towards it.

'Thank you,' I said to her. It seemed wrong, but right, to say so.

I left Farah in the room as she prepared to unwrap and dress the boy at his parents' request, and I went back along the corridor to the room where I had left my beaming new mother. Only minutes had passed, and when I opened the door and stepped back into the room's warm, damp haze, she barely registered my return. Her boy was squealing for milk and she laughed and pulled him close, teasing his lips with a bottle. His mouth found the teat and he locked on, slurping noisily as the milk dribbled over his chin and down his neck. I smiled as he guzzled the sweetness, and his mother looked up and smiled back at me. She couldn't have known where I had gone – how I had passed through shade just as her baby's arrival had brought love and light – and that was as it should have been.

The Sound

There is a sound a woman makes when she is told that her baby has died.

It is a sound that no one should ever have to make, or hear, but the midwife comes to know it well.

The sound is both human, and not. The mouth opens, but no words come out. There is only the sound: the shriek of gulls dashing shells against a jagged shore, the roar of a landslide, the groan of an iceberg as it calves, casting its mute, white offspring into the impossibly black and bottomless sea.

The sound is both powerless and powerful. In that moment, when a woman finds herself set adrift, spinning through the void, she receives the terrible knowledge that the natural order of things is a lie, and gravity an illusion. From that moment on, nothing is right, or fair. The sound the woman makes is the only thing that tethers her to the earth, and like the love she already has for the baby whose eyes will never open, the sound is strong, fierce and without end.

The sound echoes around the pale green walls of whichever windowless room the woman is in when she is told. It reverberates through the long, low-ceilinged corridors of the hospital, and ripples over the car park, and across the dual carriageway where the rush-hour traffic is gathered to listen, and out along the creeping arteries that cross the town or city.

The sound lingers, just there at the edges of the day. It hums through these words, along the page, to your fingertips, to you.

She came because she'd had a bit of a bleed. Just a few spots on her pants when she woke up. Then a little heavier when she checked again in the toilets at work, and then a clot. She would have come sooner, but she'd already had twelve days off work that year with one thing and another, and she knew her boss would have a fit if she told him she needed to leave in the middle of a busy lunch service for what he called 'another bloody check-up'. So she left it until she had bussed the last table, and swept the coins of the last lousy tip into the pockets of her apron, and then she came.

Or maybe she came because she hadn't felt the baby move since the night before. She googled what to do and she tried everything from every website and forum: a pint of cold water, loud music, a bar of chocolate, a coffee. Later, after the hospital, when she got home and began endlessly to think about why, she would feel particularly guilty about the coffee, even though her boyfriend told her not to be daft, it had nothing do to with anything she'd done.

Or maybe she came because she just knew something wasn't right. She hated phoning the hospital. She had phoned them with every ache and twinge, and the last midwife she spoke to had given her the distinct impression that she was wasting valuable time, but the thing was, her sister had had a stillbirth the previous year and she couldn't get that out of her mind. So she phoned. And she came. And something wasn't right.

Perhaps it was her first baby. Or her third. Maybe she'd already had two losses, or four, or none. She had longed for this baby, she had re-mortgaged her house for that fourth cycle of IVF, and finally it seemed to have worked, and there she was at thirty-seven weeks, so close. She had done everything right, read all the books, had finally allowed her partner to assemble the cot and the pram only the night before. Even after everything – after it was all over, and they had broken the cot one night into a pile of sticks – the pram still sat in the damp darkness of the porch, like a hunchbacked skeleton among the boots and bags.

Or perhaps she hadn't wanted the baby, barely knew the baby's dad, had thought long and hard about a termination but her mum had promised her that it would be OK, that she would help, that they would do it together. Afterwards, after everything, she blamed herself. She blamed her mum. She didn't know what to think.

She was tall with blonde hair. She was short, stout, a smoker, a drinker. A yoga enthusiast, a red-headed vegan. She was your cousin, your friend, the girl you knew at school, your desk-mate. She was that woman you used to see on the train every morning who looked pregnant, until one day she didn't.

She sat in the waiting room quite calmly. It was a busy day; there was a high-risk antenatal clinic in Outpatients that afternoon, and the consultant seemed to be sending every other woman along to Triage for further investigations. There were labourers, too: first-timers pacing the floor, clutching their TENS machines, shooting anxious glances at the staff behind the desk; and women who'd done it all before, shuttling back and forth from the toilets, trailing amniotic fluid behind them, looking at the clock on the wall and wondering if Gran and Grandpa would be willing to keep the kids another night.

She sat in the middle of this scene: still, silent, patient. She picked up a copy of *Take a Break* from the low table in front of her, thumbed through it, exchanged it for a *Staff Newsletter*, read a two-page spread about the new paediatric dialysis unit without taking any of it in. The labourers got taken ahead of her; this was only right, she thought. This visit was only a precaution. She tried to remember when she had last shaved her legs, regretted rescheduling her bikini wax, had a little argument in her head over whether to have pizza or salad for dinner. At the edge of her consciousness was a low ache – where? – somewhere at the bottom of her stomach, no, across her pelvis, even a bit uncomfortable along her thighs.

Maybe it actually wasn't fair that the others were seen before her. Maybe it had been a little too long. She looked over at the desk.

I saw her as I came out of the treatment area, glanced at her case notes long enough to read her name, and called her in.

She was in bed two. Or bed five. Or bed six. She sat back on the bed and smiled.

'Should I take my shoes off?' she asked.

'Entirely up to you,' I replied, also smiling. 'Whatever makes you comfortable.'

She swung her feet up onto the bed. She wore black zippered boots, or wedges, or slippers.

'What brings you here today?' I asked.

And she told me, and she smiled as she told me, and I smiled as I listened, and as I listened, I reached for the fetal monitor and squirted a daub of jelly onto the transducer.

'Let's have a little listen in to this baby,' I suggested. My voice was confident and casual. 'See what the wee one is up to.'

It was then that I saw the fear flicker across her face, like a fox darting through a garden at night. There, then gone. My smile may have wavered.

'Please don't worry if it takes me a few minutes to find your baby,' I said, reaching for a familiar script. 'Sometimes these rascals are tucked round a corner, or behind the placenta, and it can make them that bit harder to listen to.'

She gave a tight little nod in response to my tight little smile.

I placed the transducer against the bottom left corner of her abdomen; I don't know why I always start there, but I do, and usually the monitor's initial rustle of jelly on skin gives way to the thump, thump, thump of the fetal heart. Usually that's how it goes.

She craned her neck to see the monitor's display panel on the wall next to the bed, but there were only green and orange dashes on the screen, no numbers, and there was only static, no rhythm. I swept the transducer across her bump, firmly, steadily, a detectorist scanning for treasure on a windswept beach. I went to the curve of her hip on the right side, then up along her flank, then across the taut frame of her ribcage, then back down to where I started. I placed the transducer just above her pubic arch, I angled it this way and that. I dug. I swept. I pushed and I smiled.

She had stopped looking at the monitor now, and was looking only at me.

'What's happening?' she said.

'I'm sorry …' I began. No, I couldn't say it yet. I was sure I was only a moment away from getting it, if I just tried this angle again, if I just used a little more jelly. 'Just give me a minute.' My voice was bright and brittle.

She knew. She was looking at me, and she was listening to the syncopated heartbeats of all the other babies in all the other beds on the other side of that curtain, and she saw me for a liar. I swept and prodded in vain, but there was no foot or elbow prodding me in return, only stillness, only silence.

'I'm sorry.' This time, now, it had to be said. 'I can't find your baby's heartbeat.'

She looked at me. Everything stopped.

And then, the sound.

Afterwards, after everything, the midwife carries the sound like a stone. The weight of it is always with her, and sometimes she reaches for it willingly, turning it over, feeling its heft and smoothness, fingers searching its surface for a meaning. Every time she hears the sound, she adds another stone, each one a slightly different size and shape, until the weight is almost too much to bear – and she has built a little cairn in her heart.

Notes on Obstructed Labour

There are only so many times you can push before your body refuses. At first, when the cervix has reached full dilatation, circling the baby's head like a crown, the womb does the pushing all by itself: the muscle fibres contract, their action becoming expulsive, hurling this new life ever closer to the outside world without any conscious thought or effort on the mother's behalf. It is involuntary, automatic, primal and unstoppable. The body wants to push, and it pushes.

At the best of times, when the baby's size and position are a perfect fit with the dimensions of the mother's pelvis, and when the mother has energy and enthusiasm to spare, the pushing achieves its goal. The baby is inched further and further from inner space to outer, every hard-earned advance followed by a tiny retreat in an age-old dance of 'two steps forward, one step back', before finally, a mighty push sends the head bursting forth. There is a pause; time itself seems to hover watchfully while the mother's body gathers itself again. Then something shifts in the room – a change in the air pressure, a spatial unfolding invisible to the eye – and there is a final push. At last, the baby is cast wholly and completely out of its host, into the waiting hands of – more than likely – the midwife.

Sometimes, though, the fit is not so good, and the journey becomes long and arduous for both mother and baby. The baby is too large, or its position unfavourable; the mother's pelvis is too small, or her energy has ebbed after a labour that has already seen the sun rise and set several times. In these instances, the body's own reflexive pushes are not enough. The waves roll on and on, but they become shorter and weaker as each feeble surge yields a diminishing return. The midwife begins to tell the mother when to push, and how hard, and for how long – 'Put your chin on your chest! Now hold your breath and push into your bottom – wee bit harder, wee bit longer, wee bit harder, wee bit longer – and again –' but this incantation is often a futile prayer, and only serves to deepen the despair of the woman who has already given all she has, and more.

What happens when a woman pushes and pushes, and then is told to push and push again, until her eyes become bloodshot, and her sweat runs dry, and even her bones cry out with exhaustion? And what if this woman is wearing a cornflower-blue tunic, and an ID badge, and a fob watch? Can she still keep pushing when it becomes normal to miss her breaks, to run out of beds in which to put desperate, weeping patients, to do the work of absent colleagues who have already fallen away, clutching sick notes for stress and exhaustion? Can she push when she has missed her children's birthdays, and Parents' Night, and Christmas, when she is told again and again that she must cancel her plans and change her shifts 'to meet the needs of the service'? When her sleep is haunted by the faces of the women whose pain she could not ease, and the babies she couldn't save, and she wakes in the morning with her heart already in her throat, what then?

Leaving My Post

I wish I could say that there was one thing that did it – a disaster with a patient, or a soul-breaking bust-up with a ward sister. It would be so much easier to point to something – something outside myself, some unmistakeably painful event – and say, *Look, there it was, this is why.* You would understand. You would nod in sympathy as you read the words on the page, and you would think, *Yes, of course that's what she did. I would have done the same.*

When I arrived for my shift in Triage that evening, six of the beds in the treatment room were occupied, and there were another eight women and their angry, restless entourages in the waiting area. But the truth was, I had had busier shifts. Yes, I had also been off work earlier in the week with yet another vomiting bug whose onset had been sudden, vicious and luridly hued. Although the sickness had stopped, my stomach was still churning, and this, along with the summer sun blasting through my bedroom window, had prevented me from having my usual pre-night-shift nap. I had downed a treacle-thick coffee before leaving the house, standing jelly-limbed by the sink and tossing the mug back like a shot of tequila. The caffeine rushed through my bloodstream as I surveyed the chaos of Triage; my teeth ached and my eyes jangled with the jolt. But the truth was, I had felt worse.

Stella, the other night-shift midwife, was already at the midwives' station. I was glad to be on with her; she was unfailingly calm and kind, an anchor in the storm that surrounded us. Our eyes met over the desk, and before I could even say anything, she announced, 'We can only do what we can do. Take your time. They'll all get seen.' I tried to smile, but with the caffeine stiffening my jaw, it must have looked more like a grimace.

Betty and Madge had been on the day shift, and as the phones continued to ring mercilessly at the desk, they were already gathering their things – Betty's sequinned tote bag, Madge's cigarettes that she'd stashed in a drawer – and they gave a hurried handover as they prepared to make their exit.

'I've got beds one, five, six, and the side rooms,' Madge said. 'Bed one is a prim bleeder at eighteen weeks with fresh post-coital spotting. Beds five and six are labourers – five is a para two at term plus seven who's six centimetres with intact membranes, and six is a para one at thirty-six and six who's four centimetres, but labour ward can't take either of them yet because they've got no rooms and no midwives, so good luck with that. The first side room is a nine-week vomiter with complex social work and a needle phobia, so she's refusing IV fluids even though she's spewing rings round herself. And the other side room's a thirty-three-weeker who phoned up with severe abdo pain and diarrhoea, but she's just tanned a fish supper and fallen asleep.' She stopped and drew breath. 'Sorry, girls. We did what we could.' She was gone before we could ask for a recap.

Betty was poised with her car keys in her hand before she even began her part of the report; I could feel her desperation to leave the place behind. 'So I've got beds two, three and four,' she began. 'Bed two is an SROM from this morning who's not contracting, but she's draining grade-two meconium and starting to feel a bit unwell. The CTG's had a few early decels on it but she's another one who can't get into labour ward until they knit themselves some extra midwives.'

I glanced at Stella; her face was still carefully arranged into a semblance of calm, but I could see the worry twitching in the corners of her eyes as Betty continued her report. 'Bed three is a query cholestasis; her bloods have been sent but we're waiting for a doctor to review her results – they've all been in theatre for hours so there's no point paging them. And bed four is a prim in early labour whose boyfriend's an arse. End of story.'

'Thanks,' Stella and I said in unison, although the word was more of a formality than a genuine expression of gratitude.

'I'm on again tomorrow, so I'll see you in the morning,' Betty called over her shoulder as she disappeared through the double doors.

'Hurry back,' Stella replied, and I thought I could hear a sharp 'Ha!' from Betty as she left the unit. The incessant clatter of the phones made it hard either to hear or to think. Stella and I looked at each other.

'I'll take Madge's,' she said.

'I'll take Betty's,' I agreed.

And without another word, we began to work.

The next few hours flew by in a kind of psychedelic blur; screaming faces and splashes of blood passed in front of my eyes in endless rotation. I worked like a bastard, as the oft-used local expression would have it, but the harder I hustled, the less I seemed to accomplish. Doctors were nowhere to be seen, a shortage of staff and beds had made the labour ward impenetrable to all but the very sickest patients, women kept streaming through the doors of Triage, and the phones kept sounding their nerve-jangling alarm. Bed five delivered; Stella caught the baby while I rummaged blindly through the emergency trolley for drugs, clamps, scissors and towels. Bed six's mother was appalled by the noise. Bed four's boyfriend complained about the puddle of fluids that was seeping across the floor into his girlfriend's bed space. Bed one continued to bleed, bed two's CTG recovered from a sharp deceleration that had drummed for one heart-stopping moment above the general din, and bed three was now engaged in a very loud and animated telephone call in a language neither Stella nor I recognised. For all we knew, the side rooms were swimming in excretions of one flavour or anther – their occupants hadn't buzzed, and we'd get there eventually.

And still the phones rang at the desk. After bed five had birthed her placenta, and she and her baby had been tucked up in clean sheets, it occurred to me that maybe I should take some calls in between checking on my set of patients. Morven, the auxiliary, had been doing her best to juggle the phones so far. 'I've got five callbacks for you,' she said when I approached the desk. 'And ambulance control are on their way in with an unbooked labourer.'

I glanced down at the fob watch on my chest; apart from calling out bed five's delivery at 22.36, my concept of time had dissipated into a fog. The night had become a kind of ridiculous, Alice-in-Wonderland race in which Stella and I ran furiously on the spot, going nowhere, with no rules and no reward. The hands on my watch were creeping towards midnight. I couldn't get my head around it – what had I achieved? The waiting area was busier than when I had arrived; women paced around the chairs while their men glared at me, unblinking, their mute fury radiating across the room. I picked up one of the phones.

'Triage, Midwife Hazard speaking, how can I help you?' It occurred to me with grim irony that this standard greeting could hardly have been more apt under the circumstances. *How* can *I help you? Can I even help you at all?* I stifled a laugh.

'It's Rhona. I'm phoning for the numbers.' It was the labour-ward sister, doing her usual night-shift check on all of the departments and their bed states.

'Rhona, we've got eight patients in beds and – I don't know how many more queuing up.' I looked over at the waiting room. A woman with shocking-pink hair was pointing at me and shouting something at her partner, a muscle-bound man in a lime-green T-shirt who was rocking one of the vending machines back and forth on its stubby legs, trying unsuccessfully to dislodge one of the sugar-bombs within. When he roared in frustration, the woman roared louder, her mouth a bitter, crimson snarl. The colours were too bright, and their faces too twisted; nausea roiled the dinner that sat lumpen and undigested in my stomach.

'I don't think we'll be able to get any breaks, at this rate,' I said into the phone. 'Any chance someone could come and relieve us?'

'Not the way things are looking,' Rhona said. 'The whole place is short, so there's nowhere I can pull from. Sorry.'

'Any chance my labourers can come up? One of them's actually delivered.'

'All of our rooms are still full, and my last midwife's gone to theatre with a major haemorrhage. Sorry.'

The nausea became a slow tide of acid, climbing up my throat. Now my heart was racing, and I had a vague awareness of pins and needles in my hands. I sat down at the desk, handset cradled between my chin and shoulder. Morven had answered the other phone and was pointing at it, then at me. I shook my head.

'Rhona,' I started. What could I say? We were both powerless against the rising tide. 'Surely we need to shut the hospital.'

She sighed down the line. Closing the hospital to further admissions and diverting women to the next closest maternity unit was a last-ditch measure when things became really, truly hellish – when every single bed in the hospital was occupied, regardless of whether there were midwives to care for them. It did happen once in a very great while, but hospital bosses were incredibly loath to pull the trigger, as putting the unit on 'divert' incurred heavy fines and, occasionally, bad press. Nobody wanted to be responsible for the ensuing mess.

'You know as well as I do,' Rhona said, 'that it's out of my hands. The hospital can only close when every bed in the place is full. Which isn't the case yet.'

'But it's not safe,' I protested. My voice was small, and sounded even to me as if it were being broadcast from a great distance, like an astronaut radioing to ground control during a particularly tricky spacewalk.

'I'm sorry,' Rhona said. 'I know you're doing your best. We all are, but I don't make the rules. I wish I did. I'll call you back as soon as anything changes, and if I can send help, I will.' And she hung up.

I sat back in the chair. People kept apologising to me – Betty and Madge, then Rhona – but for what, and to what effect? The situation was beyond anyone's control. The staffing, the bed state – it had all been written in the stars, or at least sketched out long ago in an office far away by some middle manager tasked with minding the government's meagre purse, while across the area, people continued to breed. Waters broke onto bathroom floors in gushes and trickles; babies squirmed in the womb; husbands dashed through red lights while their wives groaned and pushed, jammed between back seats and footwells. Life pulsed through the city: unstoppable, terrifying, constant. My head swam with it, and for a moment, my vision began to tunnel. I blinked twice and the darkness in the corners of my eyes receded, but my pulse quickened in response.

By this point in my career, this feeling had become familiar to me: the racing heartbeat, the clammy, tingling palms, the creeping sense of dread. Was it a panic attack? Almost definitely. Was it a natural response to a job whose main prerequisite was hypervigilance – being constantly 'on', always alert for any small sign of impending crisis? Most certainly. Since that morning – now many months ago – when Trisha had fled our changing room in tears, virtually every midwife I knew had shared with me her experience of emotional turmoil. Some tales were told in jest over coffees at the desk, some in tears in the tea room. So many members of staff were on antidepressants and beta blockers that anyone who claimed to have a clean bill of mental health was more the exception than the norm. Stella herself – calm, steady Stella – had only recently mentioned in passing that she'd been on pills for years, and could barely function without them. She appeared beside me then at the desk, her white plastic apron streaked with blood.

'This is crazy,' she said. 'We need to move some of these patients through or we'll have them queuing out the door.'

I opened my mouth to say something helpful, or darkly humorous, or even just blandly reassuring, but the words dried on my tongue.

'Stella,' I began. My teeth felt clumsy in my mouth. I looked around, at the piles of call sheets and the clock on the wall, at the empty cans of energy drinks abandoned on the desk by long-departed staff, but none of it made sense. It was like a puzzle with half the pieces missing.

'Stella, I don't feel well.'

She looked down at me, her head cocked to the side. The jagged edge in my voice hadn't gone unnoticed. 'Your tummy still feeling dodgy?'

'No. I don't know,' I said, stammering. The department was at a breaking point; *I* was at a breaking point. I couldn't leave, but I couldn't work. 'Yes,' I began again. 'I think I'm going to be sick.'

Stella surveyed me coolly. She knew. And I knew that she knew. 'Go and have a seat in the tea room for a while. Take ten minutes off the floor.'

'I'm so sorry, Stella.' Another apology. 'I don't want to leave you with the place like this.'

'You're not leaving me. Morven's here. We'll be fine for ten minutes. Go.'

I didn't argue. I unfolded my limbs with a conscious effort, stood unsteadily, and marched myself into the tea room, where the door closed behind me. I was – in the midst of everything – alone. The television in the corner was showing an old episode of some game show involving two teams of families answering mildly obscene questions about each other. The host gurned a perma-tan smile; the families laughed uproariously in return. I sat down. I tried to watch the television but couldn't follow the game. I stood up, got my dinner from the fridge, and shovelled it into my mouth in under a minute: no taste, only texture. I picked up a magazine; the words swam; I put it down. I thought about going back to the desk. I had felt like this before, and had found ways of pushing it away, dampening it down, packing it up until I was home and safe and could fall quietly to pieces in the last few minutes before sleep finally silenced my thoughts. This was different, though. As I sat pinned to the tea-room chair, I felt as though my body belonged to somebody else, as if I were hovering in the corner by the telly and watching myself unhinge. My body had had a natural, normal response to the night's madness. It had been telling me to remove myself immediately, and I had refused to listen, so my brain was now taking over. *If you don't leave*, it was saying, *I will remove you from yourself.*

I tried telling myself to get a grip, to return to my post, to suck it up. I stood up, I sat down. I stood up again. I knew what I needed to do, and it killed me.

I found Stella at the desk, where she was scribbling furiously in a patient's notes, her face set with concentration.

'Stella. I need to go home.'

She looked up. I braced myself.

'Yes,' she said, looking at me. 'You need to go home.'

'I'm so sorry.' Once more, an apology. The place was awash with them. The worse things got, the sorrier we all were.

'I'll tell the coordinator,' she said. 'I'll say you came back to work too soon after your bug.'

I could have crumpled with gratitude at this small kindness. 'Thank you.'

'We'll be fine.'

'I'm so sorry.'

'I know.'

'I feel awful.'

'I know. But we're all just numbers here. Don't let it make you sick. Go.'

The phone rang again and Stella answered it. Just like that, she was involved in the story of some other woman, taking her details, listening to her pain. I hesitated. For one last moment, I had the chance to change my mind, to stay in the loop. The other phone line rang. I could have answered it. I turned and left the department.

I blinked in the darkness of the car park; shame and humiliation followed me with every step into the night. I had never been outside the building at that hour. Oblivious to the late-night drunks loitering by Accident and Emergency, I plodded towards my car. The hospital hulked at my back, humming impassively; I could still turn around, but I knew that I would not.

I drove home in silence through streets that were empty apart from an occasional ambulance, blue lights flashing towards some distant emergency. In my head, I saw the desk at Triage, saw Stella phoning Rhona to explain my departure, heard Rhona's incredulous reply. And of course, there would be gossip among the other midwives who had seen me earlier on.

'She was fine at the start of the night,' I imagined one of them saying.

'She's at it,' said another.

'She couldn't cope,' chimed a friend.

'You know what her problem is?' added another voice, and then, finally, the ultimate insult: 'She's too nice.' Ironically, this was the worst thing any midwife in my unit could say about a colleague. We all knew that in our 'caring profession', the ultimate sin was to be too soft, too kind, with a thin skin too easily needled by the challenges of our trade, and a heart too warm for its own good. The ones who lasted could be hard when it mattered, could be cold when it counted. I was learning – working on growing a little shell around myself, a cornflower-blue exoskeleton – but much as I had tried, I knew I could never be hard or cold.

Somehow, suddenly, I was home. I sat in my car outside my house as the engine ticked and cooled, and I wondered if my children would hear me coming in, and would lie rigid in their beds with fear, imagining a midnight intruder. It would never occur to them that their mother might come home in the middle of a night shift. They were used to seeing me stumble in, bleary-eyed, in the morning, saying hello and goodbye as they trundled off to school, so bright and fresh by contrast in their own clean, pressed uniforms. Now I would need to creep past their rooms, but then the comfort and safety of my own bed would be sweet relief. I could curl into my husband, could explain it all to him, and he would tell me it was fine, and I would try to believe him, and I would sleep.

As it happened, nobody heard me open the door and tiptoe up the stairs. I slipped out of my uniform on the landing and fumbled blindly for my bedroom door, and then for the edge of my bed. The sheets were cool against my skin. My husband sighed and rolled over, still asleep. I nudged him awake, and in the darkness I could see him blinking at me, uncomprehending.

'I had to come home,' I said.

'Hmmph,' he sighed again, more out of simple acknowledgement than any kind of judgement or reassurance, and closed his eyes.

'I was sick,' I said. I waited for his reply. Minutes passed, until his breathing became heavy. *I was sick*, I told myself. *I was sick*. And eventually, minutes or hours later, my own breathing steadied, and I closed my eyes, and I slept.

Going Home, and Finding the Way Back

Another hospital, in another country.

I was on the eighth floor, sitting next to a window that offered a view of the town where I grew up, its colours bleached to dust in the July heat. There were clusters of office buildings, neo-Gothic university spires and row upon row of houses, clapboard and colonial, sprawling in every direction towards the tree-lined hills. Yet from this height, within the double-glazed, air-conditioned bubble of the ward, the street-level noises were silenced and the town looked empty and still. I tilted my face into the afternoon sun and closed my eyes, like a cat. It was a rare pleasure to sit at peace in a busy hospital; my breathing barely quickened at the sound of a distant buzzer.

I sank back into my chair and enjoyed the sensation of its vinyl sticking to the backs of my thighs. This feeling reminded me of childhood road trips; long, sleepy journeys punctuated by arguments with my brother and slugs of flat strawberry soda. Reaching our destination, we had to peel our legs off the broad bench seats, our flesh bearing the perforated imprint of the leatherette upholstery for hours. I opened my eyes and was momentarily surprised and disorientated by the sight of my father sitting across from me, and then I remembered: we were both older. I was in America, and my father was sick.

Between us was a wheeled table on which my father had arranged five miniature cans of diet ginger ale. He may have been old, but he still took a boyish delight in the kinds of treats that were rare – or even forbidden – in the post-war Montreal of his childhood. The chemotherapy ward had a visitors' kitchen with an endless supply of fizzy drinks, yoghurt and Saltine crackers. My father had passed the first part of the day filling himself with every free food and beverage on offer in between casting half-hearted glances at the sports pages of the newspaper. Under the table, a towel was draped carefully over his lap. His bladder cancer, although only detected weeks before, had already had some embarrassing side effects, and the nurses had discreetly bagged the shorts he had been wearing when he arrived.

Ward staff padded back and forth across the floor, their clogs thwacking gently as they passed: another familiar sound. The curtain around our little world by the window was drawn back, and two nurses appeared with my father's next intravenous bag. They aimed the ghostly green beam of a handheld scanner at the bag's label, then at each other's badges, then at the barcode on my father's wristband. The women nodded briskly as each item in turn elicited a flash and a beep. To me, this seemed very high-tech, and in contrast made my own clinical practice seem almost quaintly old-fashioned. Whenever I checked a controlled drug or a complicated infusion with a colleague, we countersigned our names with pen and paper, and read out the handwritten numbers on our patient's ID band to confirm her identity. In fact, everything about this hospital was familiar, but fancier. As a senior academic at the university, my father was lucky to have the best private healthcare, and everything from the waterfall in the foyer, to the sushi in the canteen, to the freebies in the kitchen, spoke of money.

Regardless of the sheen of luxury, I recognised and appreciated the care my father was receiving. His diagnosis had come as a shock, and the planning and execution of his treatment had been carried out with dizzying speed. I was jet-lagged from my last-minute trip across the Atlantic and my father was tired from his own exertions, but the nurses who lingered by his chair to adjust his drip or refresh his drinks were unfailingly kind. For me, who was so used to being the carer, it was marvellous to be cared for. I felt grateful, almost embarrassingly so, for every kind word and can of ginger ale. I shifted in my armchair, mentally noting the name of every nurse for the thank-you cards I planned to write when I got home. These men and woman were going to try to fix my father, and from where I was sitting, their existence seemed nothing short of a miracle.

As I allowed myself to become absorbed in this world of comfort and kindness, a small voice spoke from the back of my mind. It began to suggest to me that perhaps I also did what these nurses were doing, albeit in a different branch of the health service, in a different country. I was struck all of a sudden by the blindingly obvious but no less mind-boggling possibility that some of my patients might feel about me the way I felt about my father's carers. Years ago, I had voluntarily placed myself slap-bang in the middle of midwifery's slipstream, the wash of bodily fluids and pain becoming so routine that disgust was soon an alien emotion. Having come so far from my first clueless shifts as a student in oversized scrubs, now it wouldn't have even occurred to me to recoil, or to wrinkle my nose. I cared for women. Clean ones, smelly ones, beautiful ones, rude ones, rich and poor ones, lost and lonely ones.

The small voice dared to become incrementally louder. *You love them,* the voice said. *You love the secrets they share and the endlessly different histories they bring to your door. You love their humour – the jokes they crack at the bleakest times, and the laughter they draw from your hoarse, aching throat as effortlessly as water from a well. You love them even when they curse and complain; you understand that pain has set their bones alight. And here's the thing: some of them love you back.* I gazed out of the window: the view was the same, still parched pale by the sun, but something in me had changed. In spite of the fact that my job had recently eked every last drop of energy and spirit from my body, I realised – almost as if the thought were occurring to someone else, in a happier echo of the out-of-body terror that had driven me, shaking, from Triage – that I was actually looking forward to getting back to work.

As I drew myself up in my chair, feeling suddenly taller, bolder, my father also shifted in his seat, setting the neatly folded newspaper down on his table. He moved carefully, trying not to upset the drip that was pulsing a steady dose of poison into his arm. 'So talk to me,' he said, looking wearily at his cannulated hand. 'This is going to take a while.'

Although my father had visited me frequently over the years in my 'new' home across the ocean, those visits had often been punctuated by distractions – happy ones, like my own children, or more irksome ones, like jet lag and illness – and I couldn't actually remember the last time we had been able to have a relaxed, unhurried conversation. It was a privilege and a delight. This was the man who used to wake up early on summer holidays to bring me blueberry muffins and apple turnovers, because they were my favourite; the man who used to tell me endless bedtime stories about a young girl who was equal parts spy, ninja, rock star and genius, and whose adventures always involved wild derring-do culminating in international fame. This man needed me now, and he wanted me to tell him some stories. Work was on my mind, and so was love – love for the women in my care, and love for my dad – so I dug deep and came up with the best tales I could tell.

Over the course of the next few hours, as the sun began to cast long shadows over our little curtained bay by the window, I told my father about some of the women who had recently passed through the Triage doors: the prims whose faces wore the naked shock of labour pain, the woman who walked calmly up to the desk with the bulge of a baby's head just visible in her trousers. I told my father about the easy, joyous births, and the long, torturous labours that left me aching for days, with a creaking back and bruises above my hips. ('Put your feet here,' I often said. 'It will give you some-thing to push against.') I told him about Eleanor and her unlikely journey to motherhood, and about perfect, pretty Jas, whose wound I had washed with tenderness. And I spoke at length about Pei Hsuan, and about the square of paper on which she had mapped out the pain and degradation of her journey to a country where she had been promised better.

My father listened in rapt silence. Nurses came to take down the empty bag of chemotherapy fluid, and to disconnect his drip, gliding away as quietly as they had appeared. The sky outside became a deeper blue as it cooled, and the city seemed to stretch and sigh with relief. Out of the corner of my eye, I saw the slow crawl of traffic, and the sway of trees.

'These stories are phenomenal,' my father said. His voice was urgent. 'You've got to write this stuff down.'

'Really?' His fascination surprised me. My father had always expressed polite interest in my work, but had never appeared to be so moved by it – or perhaps I hadn't given him the chance, hadn't bothered to share beyond a glib joke or pithy anecdote, hadn't presumed that my little world was worthy of consideration beyond the bookends of my twelve-and-a-quarter-hour shift.

'Really,' my father replied. 'People need to know about these women, and they need to know that this is what midwives do. It's – it's just amazing.'

I didn't tell my father about the toll the job had taken on me; about my racing heart, or my midnight terrors. For the first time in a very long while, I turned firmly away from the fear and the sadness. I felt uplifted by the small, strong voice in my head, and by the time spent with this man whose love for me went far beyond freshly baked muffins and bedtime stories, and by his genuine enthusiasm for what I had to say. I wanted to capture the feeling, to hold on to it, and to carry it back with me to my own hospital, in my own country, where I had chosen to live and serve.

Later that week, after the chemotherapy was finished and my father and I had embraced and whispered muffled goodbyes into each other's necks, I looked out of an aeroplane window and watched the twinkling lights of my homeland recede into darkness. When the seat-belt sign pinged off, I unlatched my tray table, dug a pen and paper out of my bag, and began to write.

The Cavalry

Those footsteps you hear are mine.

I'm running down the corridor with a bag of O-negative blood tucked under my tunic. There's a major haemorrhage in Triage and I'm hoping that my body heat will bring the fridge-fresh blood up to a comfortable temperature before it's dripped into the veins of the waxen-faced woman lying in bed three, thronged by doctors and machines. Oblivious to the staring faces that line my route, I clutch the bag to my belly, willing the woman to hold on until I return.

These are also my footsteps: the dragging plod of one battered trainer in front of another as I leave the hospital after a soul-crushing shift. I long for the sight of my family almost as much as I wish for the numbing embrace of sleep. I pass the sculpture of the pregnant woman, her bump now thickly plastered in pigeon shit, her face as inscrutable as ever, and my feet weave through the scattered debris outside the building, as they have so many times; around a gelatinous pile of sick, past the cigarette stubs and crisp packets that have settled in filthy rings around the bins. I don't know if I can do it all again the next day, and yet my heart knows that I will.

By the time you read this, I will have made that journey home and back many more times. I will have penned a dozen letters of resignation in my mind, but none will have made it onto paper. The job continues to take the best of me: my vigour, my compassion and even, at times, my health. It also continues to show me the best of what humanity can be: bold, brilliant, fearless and fierce in the face of pain and sorrow. The women in my care have taught me what it means to give love and to receive it, to triumph over unthinkable adversity and, sometimes, to accept defeat and loss with grace. For that reason, I return. I remain – in name, for now, and in my heart, for ever – a midwife.

My dedication is not exceptional, nor are my skills. I'm not the best midwife in the world – not even close. I've been in the job long enough to have an opinion, but not long enough to approach the hard-earned wisdom of so many of my senior colleagues. I can't claim to speak for every midwife everywhere. The fabric of my experience may share common threads with that of other midwives, but there will be midwives whose working environments are very different from mine, and whose feelings about the future of the maternity services are far less conflicted. There must be midwives who always feel peaceful and fulfilled at their work, whose units are well resourced and appropriately staffed, and who are able – shift after shift – to give the gold-standard, woman-centred care to which we all aspire. I just haven't met them yet. In the current climate of bed shortages and staffing shortfalls, this kind of midwife is a mythical figure – the Pegasus of our profession, her wings sprinkled with a fairy dust the rest of us can only dream of.

For the women I work alongside, and for the women we serve, I've realised that our voice – maybe even my voice – is worth raising, and that this is a story worth telling, and telling *now*. From the earliest days of my practice, I realised that the world of midwifery is so much stranger and more entertaining than fiction – hardly a day goes by when one of my colleagues doesn't marvel that 'You couldn't make this stuff up.' I imagined that I might write some of these stories down after my retirement (as others in various medical fields have done, to great effect), when hindsight may have softened some of the harder edges of my experience, and the threat of professional backlash might become somewhat moot. However, since the current government has decided that I won't be able to claim my pension until I'm sixty-seven, I have to wonder whether I'll be physically and mentally capable of practising midwifery long enough to 'retire' in the traditional sense of the word. I'm less likely to be doing night shifts and hauling beds at sixty-seven than I am to leave the profession before my knees, hips and sanity are beyond repair. Every day, my colleagues echo this concern, vowing to reduce their hours or to leave altogether as soon as mortgages are paid, debts are fulfilled, families are raised, and before the increasing desperation and fear-fuelled blame becomes too much to bear. Midwives are, on the whole, an ageing population, and if we don't let the world know how underfunded and over-burdened we are, we will never make the health service a place where the next generation of midwives can practise safely, with dignity and pride.

In some ways, I know, I shouldn't complain; I should check my privilege. I appreciate that I'm incredibly lucky to practise in a hospital with clean bedsheets, sterile instruments and a virtually endless supply of sophisticated medication, all of which are free to the user at the point of service. I know there are many midwives working around the world for whom even the most basic medical supplies are hard to come by, but that doesn't change my situation, and it won't silence my call for improvements. Regardless of what's happening elsewhere, for a maternity service in one of the world's wealthiest, most developed countries, we can and should do better for our midwives and for our women.

Sadly, the government is unlikely to prioritise this sector of healthcare until and unless there is a total sea-change in our cultural perception of midwifery and the difference midwives can make to public health – and to women like Crystal, Hawa, Olivia and Star, who span the full spectrum of circumstance and need. Even with an increasing number of depictions of midwifery in the media, there still seems to be a lack of awareness of the role's breadth and complexity, and of the almost superhuman feats of physical and psychological endurance required to carry out those duties.

This realisation dawned on a first-time father whose wife I looked after recently. Steven and Michelle had arrived in Triage with all the nervous enthusiasm of new parents-to-be. Michelle was still smiling bravely through her contractions, and Steven was juggling a set of matching suitcases while also entering crucial data into the contraction-timing app on his phone.

'I can show you the frequency, strength and duration of every contraction Michelle's had since yesterday morning,' he said, beaming as he set down the suitcases.

'Great work,' I replied, grinning. 'Now let's have a baby.'

The hospital was especially busy that day (I'm aware that this statement is a bit of a running theme, but as with every other instance heretofore, it was true). When I phoned to tell the labour ward sister that Michelle was five centimetres dilated and contracting well, she replied that the unit was desperately short-staffed, there were two obstetric theatres running, and if I brought Michelle up, I would need to stay and help her deliver her baby myself. Although this scenario meant that I would be leaving my own department short-staffed, I was given little choice. And as far as Michelle was concerned, this was the best possible outcome: she would get the same midwife in Triage and labour ward, the kind of continuity that most patients can only dream of receiving.

'There's good news and bad news,' I said to Michelle as I drew back the curtain of her bed space. She was on all fours on the bed, shuddering as a contraction eased its grip on her body. 'The good news is, I'm coming with you to labour ward. The bad news is, you're not getting rid of me.' She laughed weakly and began to climb down off the bed while Steven gathered the suitcases he'd arranged neatly at the bedside.

As it happened, Michelle had a bit of a tough time of it, and the afternoon took her on a magical mystery tour of the some of the scariest and most remote reaches of Labourland. She was in the pool, then out of it. She was on gas and air, then on diamorphine, then crying for an epidural, then back on the gas when the epidural failed to work beyond a stubbornly dense patch of numbness along her left thigh and buttock. She was off the continuous monitor, then on it, as the baby's heartbeat was steady, then stuttering. Finally, after a heroic amount of pushing, a technically 'small' but no less terrifying haemorrhage, and a complicated tear that required some tricky suturing by a particular Triage midwife who hadn't sutured in God knows how long (and whose stomach was now growling vociferously due to missing both lunch and dinner), Michelle was wrapped up in clean blankets with her beautiful baby girl.

I busied myself tidying the usual mess while they settled into their first breastfeed. As I worked my way across the room, stuffing bloodied drapes into bin bags, tossing absorbent pads onto puddles of bloody liquor, and collecting instruments that had been flung to the floor in the final moments of delivery, I became aware that Steven was watching me from his seat at Michelle's bedside. At first, I pretended not to notice, but as his eyes followed me around the room, I became uncomfortable, and smiled nervously when our gazes met.

'Sorry for staring,' he said, and I blushed at the realisation that he'd felt my unease. 'I just can't believe everything that you've done for us today. You met us in Triage, and then you came here and looked after Michelle all afternoon, and then you delivered our baby. Then you scrubbed up and did Michelle's stitches, and now you're cleaning. I keep thinking, where's the cavalry? I guess I thought there would be lots of other people in the room, or along the way, but it's just you. You're the cavalry.'

'Yup,' I said, as I lifted a bale of bloody sheets from the floor. 'I'm it.'

I tell this story not to illustrate my own brilliance; any midwife would have done the same for Michelle, and many would have done it with even greater skill and better hair. Rather, the point is Steven's revelation that midwives do so much more than catch babies. We devise and implement plans of care; we connect, console, sympathise and cheerlead; we prescribe; we do minor surgery. You see us all the way through your pregnancy, and we visit you afterwards in your home, making sure that you and your baby are well, and reminding you that cooking and cleaning and pretty much everything else can wait. When labour goes well, we're the only ones you'll see in the birthing room, and when it doesn't, we scrub for you in theatre, and then bed-bath your broken body in recovery. We believe you when you say you don't feel safe at home, and we hold you in our care until shelter is secured. We may never have met you until the day we ride into battle for you and your baby; and, like Steven, you may not even recognise the cavalry that's been at your back until the drapes are down and the blood has dried beneath your feet.

And yet, every day, in big-city hospitals and small rural birth centres, in clinics and wards, midwives of every age and stage are evaporating like so many puffs of cornflower-blue smoke. For too many of us, the pressure and exhaustion have become too much to bear. But thankfully, for every midwife who has left, thousands more of the cavalry remain: kneeling by bedsides, answering phones, running for buzzers, telling you that it's fine, you can do it, you *are* doing it – to keep pushing. And you push, and push again. And so do we.

Glossary

A note to the reader: this glossary is intended for the lay person, and uses relatively simple terms suitable for that descriptive purpose. If you would like more detailed, clinically oriented definitions, I recommend that you consult one of the many excellent professional resources available, such as Bailliere's Midwives' Dictionary, Myles Textbook for Midwives, *or* The Midwives' Guide to Key Medical Conditions.

Amnihook: A brand name for an instrument used by midwives and doctors to make a hole in the amniotic sac, or bag of waters. The instrument resembles a sterile plastic knitting needle with a hooked end, designed to snag the amniotic sac without injuring mother or baby and to allow amniotic fluid to flow out of the womb via the vagina.

Amniotic fluid: The fluid surrounding a fetus in the womb. Amniotic fluid is usually straw-coloured, and is both swallowed and excreted (as urine) by the fetus.

Amniotic sac: The sac in which a fetus grows inside the womb. Also sometimes referred to as the 'bag of waters'.

Anterior: To the front. For example, an anterior placenta is located to the front of the uterus, and a fetus's anterior shoulder is usually the first to sweep under the mother's pelvic arch in the final moments of birth.

ARM: Artificial rupture of membranes, or 'breaking the waters'; the act of breaking the amniotic sac with an instrument designed for that purpose (*see* Amnihook), often with the intention of bringing on or speeding up labour.

Auscultation: The act of listening in to the fetal heartbeat. This can be performed with a Pinard stethoscope (a small ear-trumpet which the midwife places flush against the mother's abdomen), a hand-held device using Doppler technology (*see* Doppler *and* Sonicaid), or a continuous monitor strapped to the mother's abdomen (*see* CTG).

Beat-to-beat variability: Part of a midwife or obstetrician's evaluation of a fetal heart trace (*see* CTG). A fetus whose heart trace shows prolonged, minimal beat-to-beat variability may be compromised.

BMI: Body mass index, which is calculated using an algorithm that incorporates the mother's height and weight. Women with especially low or high BMIs are sometimes regarded as 'higher risk' in pregnancy and birth.

Bradycardic: Having an unusually low pulse.

Cannula: A very thin plastic tube inserted into a vein for administration of fluids, medicines or blood.

Catheter: A tube inserted into the bladder via the urethra, for the purpose of draining the bladder. An in–out catheter is intended to be removed after the bladder is drained as a one-off event. An indwelling, or Foley's, catheter is intended to remain in the bladder and provides continuous, free drainage of urine. The latter is often used when a woman is unable to pass urine spontaneously; for example, if she is under general or epidural anaesthetic.

C. diff: *Clostridium difficile*, a bacterium that can cause severe vomiting and diarrhoea.

Cervix: Sometimes called the 'neck of the womb'. The fleshy tube which softens, thins and opens in labour to allow the fetus to pass from the uterus into the vagina.

Cholestasis: In pregnancy, a condition related to an imbalance in the liver which can cause intense itching for the mother, and an increased risk of problems for the fetus.

Colostrum: The 'first milk' produced by women after birth; nutritionally complete, highly calorific, and full of valuable immunologic substances. Many women produce colostrum in relatively small quantities in the first postnatal days; this supply can be increased by frequent breastfeeding or 'expressing', where the release of breast milk is stimulated by hand or with the aid of a device.

Contraction: A shortening of the muscle fibres within the uterus. A steady rhythm of long, strong, frequent contractions helps to soften, thin and dilate the cervix, and to expel the fetus.

Crash section: The most urgent form of Caesarean section, in which there is a clear, immediate threat to the life of mother and/or fetus. The mother is usually given a general anaesthetic so that delivery can be achieved as quickly as possible.

CTG, or cardiotocograph: A graphic representation, often either on a screen or on a paper printout, of the fetal heart rate, maternal pulse and uterine activity (contractions) over time. The term CTG is also sometimes used to describe the actual machine which produces the printout. This kind of continuous monitoring is often used to assess fetal well-being in women whose pregnancy or labour is higher-risk.

Culture bottles: Special bottles for collection of blood samples which will be sent to a lab for microbiological analysis. Where severe, systemic infection, or sepsis, is suspected, culture bottles are an essential part of the medic's diagnostic kit.

Deceleration, or 'decel': A drop in the fetal heartbeat well below the usual baseline rate. While these often form part of the fetus's normal response to labour, they can be indicative of fetal compromise.

Delirium: A mental state brought on by severe illness; can encompass confusion, disorientation and hallucinations, among other phenomena.

Diamorphine: A strong opiate drug, sometimes used for pain relief in labour.

Doppler: A term often used to describe a handheld, battery-operated ultrasound device used for auscultation of the fetal heart. *See also* Sonicaid.

Endometriosis: A condition in which endometrial tissue (which usually lines the womb) grows outside the uterus. This may lead to inflammation, pain and other problems with the internal reproductive organs.

Epidural: A form of anaesthesia in which painkilling drugs are injected into a space between the vertebrae, thus blocking the transmission of pain messages along the nerves of the spine.

Episiotomy: A cut made to widen the vaginal opening at birth. Although episiotomies used to be a routine part of obstetric practice, now they are usually only done for very specific reasons; for example, to speed up the final moments of delivery if the fetus is believed to be in danger, or to allow the introduction of forceps.

Facial oxygen: Medical shorthand for pure oxygen which is administered to a patient using a facemask or nasal tubes; often administered in episodes of acute illness, such as sepsis.

Fallopian tubes: Two slim tubes leading from the ovaries to the uterus.

Fetal scalp electrode: An instrument which can be connected to the fetal scalp in labour to monitor the fetal heart more accurately than a trans-abdominal CTG.

Fetus: The medical term used to refer to a baby at any time between eight weeks of pregnancy and the moment of delivery.

Forceps: An instrument for delivering babies in situations where the mother's cervix is fully dilated, but the progress of labour thereafter becomes inappropriately slow and/or the fetus's condition is compromised. The instrument comprises two large, interlocking spoons or 'blades'; these are positioned around the fetus's head by the operator (usually a doctor) and traction is then applied in conjunction with the mother's pushing in order to achieve delivery.

Fully dilated: An expression which refers to the cervix being fully open, usually approximately 10 centimetres in diameter. Generally speaking, this stage must be reached before a fetus can be born vaginally.

Haemorrhage: Excessive blood loss. This can occur at any stage of pregnancy, labour or the postnatal period for a number of reasons.

High dependency: The area of the labour ward where critically ill women are cared for, with increased midwifery and medical attention as well as additional monitoring.

Hypnobirthing: The brand name of a style of antenatal education which focuses on the woman's innate ability to have a spontaneous, pain-free labour and birth. Hypnobirthing encourages the use of breathing, affirmations and visualisation to reduce or eliminate pain in labour. In this style of birthing, contractions may be referred to as 'surges'.

Hypotensive: Having low blood pressure.

Internal examination: Also referred to as a 'vaginal examination', or VE. An examination in which the practitioner (midwife or doctor) uses her fingers to feel the length, consistency and dilatation of the cervix. The examiner may also be able to determine whether the amniotic sac is intact, whether the baby is presenting feet- or head-first, and the position and descent of the presenting part. Many guidelines suggest that these examinations should be done at least every four hours in labour, as they can yield information which guides the midwife or doctor's management; however, the frequency of internal examinations varies widely in practice, depending on the clinical situation, the woman's wishes, and the shared decision-making of patient and practitioner.

In utero: Latin for 'in the uterus' or 'in the womb'.

IOL, or induction of labour: A process of artificially initiating labour using a number of stages and techniques, often including ARM (*see above*) and the administration of synthetic hormones using both vaginal pessaries and intravenous drips.

IV, or intravenous: Referring to a drug or fluid which is administered directly into the veins, usually through a cannula or 'drip' in the hand or arm.

Labia: The fleshy folds of skin, or 'lips', of a woman's external genitalia.

Liquor: *See* Amniotic fluid.

Malposition: A situation in which the fetus's position in the womb makes vaginal delivery difficult or impossible.

Meconium: The thick, tarry substance produced by the fetus's gut; a primitive, sterile faeces. Sometimes the fetus passes meconium during pregnancy or labour, and the amniotic fluid is said to be 'meconium-stained'. This can be a normal event but can also indicate fetal compromise.

Missed miscarriage: An instance in which a fetus of less than twenty-four weeks' gestation has died, but no blood or tissue has yet been passed, giving the impression of a continuing pregnancy.

Mucus plug: *See* Show.

Obs and gyn(ae): The commonly used shorthand term for obstetrics (the medical speciality pertaining to pregnancy, birth and the postnatal period) and gynaecology (the medical speciality pertaining to the female reproductive organs and their surrounding structures). Doctors often specialise in the combined fields of obstetrics and gynaecology, rather than one or the other in isolation.

Ovary: A reproductive organ which produces eggs and hormones (progesterone and oestrogen); in normal anatomy, there are two ovaries, each one linked to the uterus by a fallopian tube.

Paediatrician: A doctor who specialises in infants and children.

Palpation: In midwifery, the systematic process of feeling a woman's abdomen to assess (among other things) the size, lie, presentation and position of the fetus, and the strength and frequency of contractions.

Parous, or 'para': Generally speaking, this refers to a woman who has previously given birth to a baby of twenty-four weeks' gestation or more, or to a baby of less than this gestation who lived more than momentarily. A number can then be added to this description: for example, a 'para one' is a woman who has previously had a baby of viable gestation; a 'para four' is a woman who has had four babies of viable gestation, a 'para one plus two' is a woman who has had one baby of viable gestation as well as two other pregnancies.

Perinatal: Relating to the time around birth; for example, perinatal mental health refers to issues which may arise in pregnancy and/or the postnatal weeks or months.

Perineum: The area between the vaginal opening and the anus.

***Per vaginam* (PV):** Latin for 'by way of the vagina'. Vaginal secretions such as amniotic fluid and menstrual blood can be said to come *per vaginam*, or PV.

Pinard: a simple instrument used for listening to the fetal heart. Shaped like the end of a small trumpet, Pinards were widely utilised before the invention of Sonicaids and CTGs, and are still sometimes used in clinics and rural or low-risk settings.

Placenta: The organ which forms in pregnancy to transfer nourishment and oxygen from the mother to the fetus. The placenta implants on the wall of the uterus and is expelled in the third stage of labour, after the delivery of the baby; hence its nickname as the 'afterbirth'.

Placenta praevia: A condition in which the placenta encroaches on or covers the internal opening of the cervix, making vaginal delivery dangerous for both mother and baby.

Post-coital: After sexual intercourse.

Post-dates: Relating to a pregnancy which has continued past 'term', or forty weeks' gestation.

Posterior: To the back. For example, a baby's posterior shoulder is to the back of the mother and is usually the second shoulder to be delivered at birth. A posterior placenta is implanted on the back of the lining of the uterus.

Postpartum haemorrhage (PPH): Excessive blood loss after birth; usually accepted as anything over 500 millilitres. This can be caused or exacerbated by a number of things, including trauma to the genital tract, failure of the uterus to contract properly after delivery, or a shortage of essential clotting factors in the bloodstream.

Pre-eclampsia: A condition of pregnancy which is usually characterised by high blood pressure, swelling and protein in the urine. Left untreated or poorly controlled, pre-eclampsia can be fatal for both mother and fetus.

Primigravida, or 'prim': A woman who is pregnant for the first time.

Prostin: A commonly used brand of hormone pessary, often inserted towards the back of the vagina in the first stage of induction of labour with the aim of softening, shortening and opening the cervix.

Pyrexia: Fever; a temperature above the upper limit of normal (roughly 37.5 degrees Celsius).

Query: In medical terminology, used as a prefix to a medical condition in order to denote a degree of uncertainty about the diagnosis. For example, 'query cholestasis' would indicate a tentative but unproven diagnosis of cholestasis.

Recovery: An area of the labour ward usually reserved for post-operative care; for example, a woman who has had a Caesarean section will usually spend several hours in Recovery before being transferred to a postnatal ward.

Rectal pressure: A sensation similar to the need for a bowel movement, caused by the fetus's presenting part descending through the pelvis and putting pressure on the mother's pelvic floor. This feeling often precedes or accompanies the urge to push.

Registrar, or 'reg': In the UK, a doctor who has completed two years of foundation training and is now at least two years into their period of specialist training. In British obstetrics and gynaecology, specialist training generally takes seven full-time years, after which the doctor is eligible to become a consultant.

Resuscitaire: A brand name for a large device or machine used for warming and resuscitation of babies at birth; usually allows for the administration of oxygen and suction, as well as the storage of other essential instruments and drugs used in neonatal resuscitation.

Rigours: Full-body shivers caused by the body's attempts to regulate its temperature during serious infection or sepsis.

Ruptured ectopic: An ectopic pregnancy is one that occurs outside the main body of the uterus, typically in one of the Fallopian tubes; a 'ruptured ectopic' occurs when an ectopic pregnancy outgrows the structure in which it is contained. This frequently leads to life-threatening bleeding and requires immediate surgical attention.

Senior house officer, or 'SHO': An outdated but still commonly used term for a doctor who is either in their second year of foundation training (*see* Registrar), or in their first one or two years of specialist/GP training; the rank below a registrar.

Sepsis: A life-threatening complication of infection which can compromise the body's vital organs and, ultimately, cause death. Sepsis continues to be one of the leading causes of maternal and neonatal death and, as such, is treated as an emergency.

Show: Also called the 'mucus plug'; the thick, jelly-like substance which seals the cervix during pregnancy and is often expelled as labour begins and progresses.

Sliding scale: A carefully titrated system of administering glucose and insulin simultaneously via pump infusion to regulate the body's blood-sugar level; often used for diabetic patients in labour.

Sonicaid: A brand name for a handheld device used to listen to the fetal heartbeat; *see also* Doppler.

Speculum: An instrument, usually plastic, used for holding the vaginal walls apart in order to visualise the vagina and cervix. This can be useful when trying, for instance, to determine the cause of bleeding, or the presence of amniotic fluid.

Spines: The shorthand term for ischial spines, bony prominences within the pelvis which are often used as landmarks to determine fetal descent in labour. For example, a fetus whose presenting part (usually the head) can be felt 2 centimetres below the mother's ischial spines may be described as 'spines plus two'.

SROM: Spontaneous rupture of membranes; when the mother's 'waters break' on their own.

Stat: Immediately. From the Latin, *statim*.

Stillbirth: A baby born after twenty-four weeks of pregnancy which has not shown any signs of life at delivery.

Syntocinon: A brand name for a synthetic version of oxytocin, the hormone which causes the uterus to contract. Syntocinon is used for a number of reasons, including induction of labour and acceleration of a labour which has slowed or stalled.

Tachycardia: An abnormally fast heartbeat; in pregnant women, this is generally accepted to be a pulse above 100 beats per minute. In fetuses, over 160 beats per minute.

TENS: Transcutaneous electrical nerve stimulation; the term often used to describe a machine comprising a battery pack and electrode leads which are applied to the patient's back with the aim of blocking pain signals in labour.

Term: Full gestation of pregnancy: forty weeks. A woman who is said to be at 'term plus eight' is eight days past her due date.

Third-degree tear: A childbirth-related tear involving one or both of the anal sphincter muscles as well as perineal skin and muscle, often described in layperson's terms as 'a tear that involves the back passage'. Third-degree tears are usually repaired in theatre by a doctor, with the patient under spinal or epidural anaesthetic.

Trial of forceps: An attempt to deliver a baby with the use of forceps where success is uncertain.

A trial of forceps is almost always undertaken in the operating theatre: if the trial is unsuccessful, all of the necessary staff and instruments are immediately available to perform a Caesarean section.

Unbooked: Relating to a woman who has not yet accessed antenatal care within the local area. For example, an 'unbooked labourer' is a woman who is unknown to the local maternity service, but is now presenting in labour.

Ureters: Tubes which carry urine from the kidneys to the bladder.

Uterine activity: A term often used in clinical documentation to denote contractions. For example, 'uterine activity 2 in 10' describes an average frequency of two contractions in ten minutes.

Uterus: The womb; the organ in which the fetus grows.

Vagina: The fleshy internal passage which leads from the cervix to the exterior of the body.

Ventouse: Also known as a vacuum extractor; an alternative to forceps (*see above*). A suction cup which is applied to the fetus's head, allowing traction (and, in certain circumstances, rotation) to be applied.

Vernix: The thick, pasty substance that protects the fetus's skin in the womb and may still be found on the baby in varying quantites at the time of birth.

Vertex: An area on the top of a baby's head which, in a normal vaginal birth, is usually the first part to descend or 'present'.

Viable: Likely to survive. Current law states that fetuses of twenty-four weeks' gestation or over are viable, although an increasing number of babies born before that time are surviving with the aid of advanced neonatal care.

VSD: Ventricular septal defect; a common congenital (present from birth) heart defect.

Vulva: The external female genitalia; often referred to incorrectly as the vagina.

... and a Note on Gender

Birth stays the same, but society changes. I recognise that some birthing parents do not self-identify as women and that an increasing number of midwives nowadays are men. However, in my (admittedly limited) experience, every mother and midwife I have encountered has self-identified as female, so I have referred to them here as such. It should go without saying that the hopes and aspirations I've expressed for the women in this book apply equally to all midwives and pregnant parents, regardless of label or gender.

Acknowledgements

To every agent and editor who welcomed this book in its most primitive form with unmitigated enthusiasm and warmth: thank you for showing me that my story was worth telling and for expressing your love and admiration for the work that midwives do. Each and every one of you is remembered and appreciated.

Thank you to Hayley Steed, agent extraordinaire and future chief executive of a global publishing empire; thank you for believing in me and my fellow midwives, for spreadsheeting my existence with breathtaking precision and for humouring my steady stream of dog photos. You deserve all the champagne, not just for birthdays and barbecues. And thank you to the whole Madeleine Milburn Agency team, for bearing with me as I blunder through the industry for the very first time and for having my back along the way.

Thank you to Sarah Rigby, my wonderful editor, for understanding from the outset where I wanted my story to go, and for guiding me with unflappable patience and skill. You've (almost) persuaded me that I'm an Author with a capital A and I'm proud to call you a Friend with a capital F. To Jocasta Hamilton and all at Hutchinson and Cornerstone: thank you for welcoming me to your world and for your total commitment to my work from that very first meeting. Special thanks to Laura Brooke, Elle Gibbons and Sarah Ridley for pushing hard and to Sasha Cox for being my first superfan.

Huge gratitude to Susan Roan and Gareth Reid for joining me in the journey from doula to midwife to author (and friend) and for being unwaveringly enthusiastic and supportive through it all.

My heartfelt thanks to midwife Erin Hutchings and obs/gynae consultant Adam Archibald for providing invaluable 'insider' feedback, which was gentle, thoughtful and so very much appreciated.

To every midwife who has mentored me, knowingly or unknowingly, from training right through to today: thank you for leading by strong, graceful, foul-mouthed, huge-hearted example. You have shown me how to be 'with women': a gift I can only pay forward. And to all of my colleagues in the extended NHS family – the doctors, auxiliaries, porters, domestics and clerical staff who have taught me, supported me and saved my bacon in 'this place' on countless occasions – thank you.

To the women who have allowed me to care for them in times of the greatest joy and the deepest pain, and to their families: there is no greater privilege. For your generosity of time and spirit, for your strength and your wit: a debt of gratitude and love. Midwives work hard, but the work of motherhood is so much harder.

To family on both sides of the Atlantic: thank you for your unstinting support. And finally, to my own little family: words aren't enough. To my husband, Alan, who is my greatest fan and my own personal midwife: your love and your time are the greatest gifts of all. To my girls, the most amazing women I know: it's all for you.

Leah Hazard is an actively serving NHS midwife. Having studied at Harvard, she left a career in television to pursue her lifelong interest in women's health after the birth of her first daughter. She soon began working as a doula, supporting women in pregnancy and attending numerous births in homes and hospitals across the country. The birth of Leah's second daughter prompted her to make the leap into midwifery. Since qualifying, she has worked in a variety of clinical areas within the NHS maternity services, including antenatal clinics, triage units and labour wards.